At Home

with Natalie

At Home

with Natalie

SIMPLE RECIPES *FOR* HEALTHY LIVING *FROM* MY FAMILY'S KITCHEN *TO* YOURS

NATALIE MORALES

with **ANN VOLKWEIN**

PHOTOGRAPHY BY **ALANNA HALE**

HOUGHTON MIFFLIN HARCOURT
BOSTON   NEW YORK   2018

Library of Congress Cataloging-in-Publication Data
Names: Morales, Natalie, author. | Volkwein, Ann, author.
Title: At home with Natalie : simple recipes for healthy living from my
family's kitchen to yours / Natalie Morales with Ann Volkwein.
Description: Boston : Houghton Mifflin Harcourt, 2018. | Includes index.
Identifiers: LCCN 2017059029 (print) | LCCN 2017051879 (ebook) | ISBN
9780544974562 (ebook) | ISBN 9780544974494 (paper over board)
Subjects: LCSH: Cooking. | Nutrition. | LCGFT: Cookbooks.
Classification: LCC TX714 (print) | LCC TX714 .M6668288 2018 (ebook) | DDC
641.5—dc23
LC record available at https://lccn.loc.gov/2017059029

Book design by JENNIFER K. BEAL DAVIS

Printed in China
TOP 10 9 8 7 6 5 4 3 2 1

To my family, friends, and

the fans who have supported me

so much through the years

Contents

Introduction

THE ONE CONSTANT IN LIFE IS CHANGE.
And the feeling that one is home has little to do with a house—or even a country. These are lessons I learned from a very young age. My father's job in the air force kept us always on the move. On average, every three years we would set off on a new adventure. During my first eighteen years, we moved eight times, hopping from where I was born in Taiwan to places like Panama, Brazil, Spain—and we even had a few years in the United States. Fortunately for my two sisters and me, we grew up seeing the world. And I often say my childhood was what led me to my career as a journalist. Once I had a little of that wanderlust in me, it sparked my curiosity to see and do whatever the world had to offer. My love of travel, experiencing cultures, and learning languages are what grounded me, in a way. But more so, they shaped me into the person I am today.

When I started the process of writing this cookbook, once again I found myself at a crossroads. After fifteen years (the longest I have ever lived anywhere) in one place, Hoboken, New Jersey, my job was moving me across the country to Los Angeles, to become both the West Coast

ABOVE, LEFT TO RIGHT:

My abuelita Tita, my mother, me in her arms, my dad, and my sister Patricia in Guajataca (near Arecibo), Puerto Rico c. 1973 • My mom, my sister Patricia, and me at the Spanish ruins, Panama City, Panama c. 1977 • Back row: Patricia, my mom, Abuelita Tita, Abuelito Mario. Seated: Me and my sister Priscilla on my eleventh birthday, Dover, Delaware c. 1983 • Priscilla, me, and Patricia in Piazza San Marco, Venice, Italy c. 1987

anchor of the *TODAY* show and the host of *Access Hollywood*. I'd always dreamed of living in California at some point in my life, as had my husband, and I thought the change of pace would be good for our family. But . . . my kids were both born and raised in Hoboken. They'd had a completely stable world in one place, and were none too sure about the move. I reassured the boys that life brings us change, and not always good or exciting change, but that in moving as a family we bring the comforts of home with us. And those things allow us to find ourselves again, and to grow, and, eventually, establish new roots. Home is indeed where the heart is.

Needless to say, when we arrived in California I found myself channeling my mother's ability to create home wherever we were. Growing up, I always found comfort in the kitchen. No matter whether I'd had a good or a bad day at school, once I walked in the door, I was greeted with the familiar aroma of something frying, roasting, or baking. I would often join my mom at the stove or kitchen table ready to help chop, stir, or

even just put out the place settings. No matter where we were, our family dinners (even if we were in a hotel for months between moves) allowed us to feel at home.

The simple act of gathering around the table, with no distractions or cell phones, is such a powerful, bonding experience. I know, of course, it's not always possible. My kids have lots of sports and after-school activities, and my husband and I travel for work on occasion, so it's not every day that we can sit down as a family. But we do manage to gather together a few nights during the week, and especially on the weekends. It's that family time, holding hands saying a prayer and telling stories at the dinner table, that centers us.

That is where this cookbook comes in—it's born from my many years side by side with my mom and sisters, helping cook many of the foods of our Brazilian and Puerto Rican heritage. Also featured are recipes my family and I adopted as favorites in the many places we lived in or traveled to. I learned to cook largely through osmosis, which is a good thing,

ABOVE, LEFT TO RIGHT:

Me with Duke the dog, my mom, Patricia, and Dad at Miraflores Locks, Panama Canal Zone, Panama c. 1977 • Priscilla, me, Mom, and Patricia at Sacré-Coeur, Montmartre, Paris, France c. 1986 • Patricia, me, and Mom in front of our house and Mitsubishi Colt, Taichung, Taiwan c. 1972 • Vovo Daria with Patricia and my mother and me in Rio de Janeiro c. 1978

because any time I try to ask my mother how she makes a signature dish, she tells me roughly a little of this and a little of that, but it's never really right on paper, or tested. Hidden in her stacks and stacks of recipe index cards, with handwritten notes, torn out magazine pages with recipes, and cookbooks she hardly ever touches are a treasure trove of our own family favorites, buried deep in memories.

There is so much family history in the food we make in my house. Whether it's my late grandmother's Arroz con Pollo y Gandules (page 96) from Puerto Rico, or my mother's empanadas (page 66) or flan (page 262), these are recipes that need to be recorded, preserved, and passed on, to be enjoyed by new friends and their families. And these are the foods of my many homes, in many countries, over the years. If, as they say, variety is the spice of life, here you will find a very global perspective with both healthy and indulgent options. I hope you enjoy creating your own memories and family time, from my family's table to yours.

Power-Up Breakfasts

I am a big breakfast eater and really can't function without a little something before heading off to work or getting started with the day. The problem is, usually I am getting up a little after four A.M., and I don't have a lot of time to cook or eat, not to mention much of an appetite. But one of the things I like to do, to cut down on any prep time, is plan a bit ahead or even make things over the weekend that I know will make for a perfect grab-and-go breakfast throughout the week. If I'm going to have a very busy day, I'll make sure to take extra for later in the morning when I know I will need to refuel. So here are some of my go-to breakfasts that will keep you powered up all day long.

10-MINUTE MUFFIN FRITTATA

GLUTEN-FREE
MAKES 12

Nonstick cooking spray

6 large eggs

¼ cup (whole or 2%) milk

1 tablespoon fresh chives or
½ teaspoon dried chives

Salt and freshly ground
black pepper

½ cup grated mozzarella cheese

⅓ cup chopped ham or
crumbled cooked bacon

¼ cup minced yellow onion

¼ cup finely chopped spinach
or broccoli

I KNOW—of course you don't even have 10 minutes to make a frittata most mornings! The secret here: Make them ahead, then reheat and go all week. Or prepare the frittata mix the night before, then just give it a stir, pour into a muffin tin, and bake. These are also a way to sneak protein and vegetables into your kids before they head to school . . . Any extras make for a filling midmorning, afternoon, or after-school snack.

1. Preheat the oven to 375°F. Lightly grease a 12-cup muffin tin with nonstick spray.

2. In a large bowl, whisk together the eggs, milk, chives, and salt and pepper to taste. Stir in the mozzarella, ham, onion, and spinach.

3. Pour the egg mixture into the prepared muffin tin. Bake until the eggs are set in the middle, about 10 minutes.

Variation For a full-size frittata, use an 8-inch oven-safe skillet or pie dish. Coat all sides with nonstick spray, then pour in the egg mixture. Bake at 375°F until the middle is set, about 20 minutes.

EGG AVOCADO BOAT

GLUTEN-FREE
VEGETARIAN
SERVES 1

1 avocado, halved and pitted

2 medium eggs

1 teaspoon extra-virgin olive oil

Pinch of salt

Pinch of freshly ground
black pepper

1 tablespoon chopped fresh
chives or cilantro (optional)

Salsa, hot sauce, or freshly
grated Parmesan cheese
(optional)

I LOVE EGGS AND AVOCADO, and especially the combination of the two together. Notice that when you take the pit out of the center of an avocado, you have an indentation almost exactly the size of an egg yolk. This is such a protein- and omega-3-rich breakfast (or lunch), and it keeps me satiated for hours.

You do have to make this right before eating, but it takes no more than 15 minutes and is well worth it. Just sprinkle with a little hot sauce, fresh herbs, and/or any condiment of your choosing and serve with a side of whole-grain toast or tortillas to mop up the perfectly runny yolks.

1. Preheat the oven to 450°F.

2. Scoop out some of the avocado flesh from each half to make more room for the egg. Put the avocados side by side in a baking dish (if they are having trouble stabilizing, cut just a little off the back of the avocado so it sits flat). Gently break an egg into the center of each avocado. Drizzle with the olive oil and season with the salt and pepper.

3. Bake until the whites are fully cooked and the yolks look set but still a little runny, 10 to 12 minutes.

4. Remove from the oven and garnish with chopped chives and salsa, hot sauce, or Parmesan, if desired.

BREAKFAST QUINOA BOWL
with Swiss Chard & Chicken Maple Sausage

SERVES 1

2 to 3 chicken maple breakfast sausage links, cut into slices

1 tablespoon extra-virgin olive oil

¼ cup diced yellow onion

¼ cup chopped mushrooms

½ cup chopped Swiss chard or kale leaves or prewashed baby kale

1 cup cooked quinoa (prepared according to the package instructions)

Salt and freshly ground black pepper

1 tablespoon chopped fresh cilantro (optional)

Hot sauce (optional)

ANOTHER PERFECT BREAKFAST you can make in under 10 minutes, and it will keep you going all day! The key here is precooked quinoa. I usually make a pot of quinoa on weekends and then use it throughout the week in salads or mixed in with lots of protein and vegetables, like this breakfast bowl. You can even add a sunny-side-up egg for even more protein and omega-3 fats.

1. In a skillet, cook the chicken sausage over medium-high heat until browned and thoroughly cooked, 5 to 6 minutes. Remove from the pan and set aside.

2. In the same pan, heat the olive oil over medium-high heat. Add the onion and mushrooms and cook, stirring, until softened, about 2 minutes. Stir in the Swiss chard and cook, stirring, until it's wilted but still green, about 1 minute more.

3. Stir in the quinoa and cooked sausage, mixing with all the vegetables. Season with salt and pepper.

4. Sprinkle with cilantro and add a dash of hot sauce, if desired, and serve.

EGG & SAUSAGE STRATA

SERVES 8 TO 10

1 pound low-fat turkey (or chicken) Italian sausage

½ cup diced yellow onion

12 large eggs

1 cup whole or 2% milk

1 cup half-and-half

2 teaspoons salt

Pinch of freshly ground black pepper

Pinch of cayenne pepper

1 pound baby spinach

6 asparagus spears, chopped

1 (12-ounce) package shredded cheese (I prefer the cheddar, Monterey Jack, and mozzarella mix, but use the cheese of your choosing)

¼ cup minced fresh chives

1 tablespoon chopped fresh oregano, or 1 teaspoon dried oregano

1 loaf day-old bread (preferably a country or hearty bread), cut into cubes

Nonstick cooking spray

2 tablespoons freshly grated Parmesan cheese

THIS IS A DELICIOUS CASSEROLE my mother makes on many holiday mornings. It can all be premade the night before and popped in the oven in the morning. The whole house will wake up to the fragrant smell of this amazing breakfast strata. The best part is it's versatile—and can put any leftover stale bread or vegetables to good use.

---

1. In a large skillet, combine the sausage and onion and cook over medium-high heat, stirring and breaking up the sausage, until the sausage is no longer pink, 6 to 8 minutes. Refrigerate until ready to use.

2. Crack the eggs into a large bowl. Whisk in the milk and half-and-half. Season with the salt, black pepper, and cayenne. Stir in the spinach, asparagus, shredded cheese, chives, and oregano. Stir in the bread cubes and allow everything to soak overnight, covered, in the refrigerator, or for at least a few hours.

3. Preheat the oven to 350°F. Coat a 9 by 13-inch baking dish with nonstick spray.

4. Pour the bread, vegetable, and egg mixture into the baking dish. Top with the sausage and onion and sprinkle with the Parmesan.

5. Bake until the strata is set, about 45 minutes. If you prefer a more golden top, broil for just 1 minute. Let cool slightly, then serve.

AVOCADO, PARMESAN & TOMATO TOAST

VEGETARIAN
SERVES 1

1 ripe avocado, halved and pitted

2 slices whole wheat bread

2 teaspoons extra-virgin olive oil

1 plum tomato, thinly sliced

Freshly ground sea salt
and black pepper

½ teaspoon Tajín Clásico
seasoning

½ teaspoon freshly grated
or thinly sliced Parmesan cheese

THIS IS ONE OF MY FAVORITE BREAKFASTS, especially on mornings when I'm trying to get on the road in 5 minutes. Honestly, this will take you no more than the time to toast the bread and cut the avocado. It is nutritious, filling, and a great meal to take with you as you walk out the door. (I should know, as I'm usually juggling a coffee cup in one hand and the avocado toast in the other.) I also feel that if I start my day with something wholesome and filling like this, it sets me up for a good day of eating right without processed or sugary foods. This recipe calls for Tajín, a chili, lime, and sea salt spice available in the Latin foods aisle.

1. Slice into the flesh of the avocado (but not through the skin), creating long, thin sections, then scoop out the avocado slices.

2. Toast the bread slices to your liking, then drizzle the toast slices with the olive oil.

3. Shingle the tomato slices on the toast, then season them with a pinch each of salt and pepper. Layer the avocado on top of the tomatoes, then sprinkle evenly with the Tajín seasoning. Lightly sprinkle the Parmesan on both pieces of avocado toast and serve.

EFFORTLESS BUCKWHEAT PANCAKES

GLUTEN-FREE
VEGETARIAN
MAKES ABOUT
TWELVE 5-INCH
PANCAKES

1¼ cups buckwheat flour
(or if you don't care to be gluten-free,
try ¾ cup buckwheat flour
and ½ cup all-purpose flour)

2 tablespoons sugar

1 teaspoon baking powder

1 teaspoon baking soda

1 large egg

2 tablespoons vegetable oil

½ teaspoon pure vanilla extract

2 cups buttermilk

2 tablespoons unsalted butter
or nonstick cooking spray,
for the griddle

THE FIRST TIME I MADE THESE PANCAKES, I thought, *There's no way my kids will eat them*, because they look too healthy, are brownish in color, and aren't fluffy or cakey like the pancakes they love. But then I thought, *Let's give them a try*. Well, my son Josh asks for these pancakes over any other pancake now. I think it's because they are light but the buckwheat gives them a nutty flavor, and they soak up whatever you put on them.

My boys love Nutella on top of anything, but these are delicious with a fruit compote, light jam, or syrup, too. And you can feel good that they are good for you, gluten-free, and pretty simple to make.

1. Preheat a griddle over medium heat.

2. In a large bowl, whisk together the flour, sugar, baking powder, and baking soda.

3. In a small bowl, whisk together the egg, oil, vanilla, and 1 cup of the buttermilk. With a spatula, stir the egg mixture into the flour mixture until well blended.

4. Slowly add the remaining 1 cup buttermilk, mixing until you reach the right consistency—you want it to be the thickness of paint, and you may not use all of it—and the batter is smooth. There may be a few lumps, but that's fine.

Note: These freeze beautifully, so make up a batch and you've got breakfast ready all week.

5. Lower the heat under the griddle to medium-low. Coat the griddle with butter, and when the butter is hot, ladle the batter into 5-inch disks on the griddle.

6. When the pancakes start to bubble on the surface or the bottom side seems cooked, about 3 minutes, flip and cook until browned on the second side, 1 to 2 minutes more. Use more butter as needed between batches.

BURRITO with Eggs, Black Beans & Canadian Bacon

SERVES 1

2 large eggs

2 tablespoons whole or 2% milk

Salt and freshly ground black pepper

2 tablespoons extra-virgin olive oil

3 Canadian bacon slices

¼ cup diced yellow onion

½ cup canned black beans, drained and rinsed

1 large flour tortilla

Salsa or pico de gallo (optional)

MAKE THIS BURRITO AHEAD and just reheat when you're ready to eat. I do prefer making these burritos fresh, though, and you'll see they really don't require too much in the way of time or preparation. I make these as individual servings, but fry up all the Canadian bacon, cook a whole can of beans, and prepare as many scrambled eggs as you'll need and you can easily make burritos for the whole family.

1. In a small bowl, whisk the eggs and milk together. Season with a pinch each of salt and pepper.

2. In a medium skillet, heat 1 tablespoon of the olive oil over medium-low heat. Add the egg mixture and cook, stirring occasionally with a rubber spatula, until just firm and scrambled, about 3 minutes. Transfer from the skillet to a plate.

3. In the same skillet, cook the Canadian bacon over medium-high heat until golden and crisp on the edges, about 4 minutes.

4. In a separate small skillet, heat the remaining 1 tablespoon olive oil over medium-high heat. Add the onion and cook, stirring, until starting to soften, 1 to 2 minutes. Stir in the black beans and season with a pinch each of salt and pepper. Remove from the heat.

5. Heat the flour tortilla in the microwave for about 20 seconds.

6. Assemble on the tortilla: Start with the Canadian bacon, then add the scrambled eggs, and top with the black beans. Roll the burrito tightly and serve with a side of salsa or pico de gallo, if desired.

BANANA CHIA PUDDING

GLUTEN-FREE
VEGETARIAN
SERVES 2

2 bananas, cut into thirds

1½ cups almond milk, soymilk, or flax milk

⅓ cup chia seeds

¼ cup honey or agave nectar

1 teaspoon pure vanilla extract

½ teaspoon ground cinnamon

Pinch of salt

2 tablespoons finely chopped almonds or walnuts, for garnish (optional)

Note: This recipe requires a few hours to chill and set.

I LIKE TO MAKE THIS, another perfect breakfast or snack for super busy mornings, the night before and chill it overnight. It's also delicious as a warm pudding; just heat it in the microwave right before eating. Banana and chia are a power combo, filling you up and giving you plenty of energy.

1. In a blender, combine the bananas, milk, chia seeds, honey, vanilla, cinnamon, and salt. Blend until smooth.

2. Pour the mixture into two pint-size mason jars and chill overnight, or for at least a few hours, to allow the chia to thicken into a pudding. Top with the almonds, if desired.

3. If you like it cold, just spoon it out and enjoy. If not, heat it for a minute in the microwave for a warm, creamy banana pudding.

Variation For a chocolaty pick-me-up, add 1 tablespoon unsweetened cocoa powder with the other ingredients in Step 1 and blend.

PURE POWER WAFFLES

GLUTEN-FREE
VEGETARIAN
MAKES ABOUT
5 WAFFLES

Nonstick cooking spray

1 cup gluten-free flour blend
for waffles (I like Pamela's, which
uses ¾ cup water, 1 large egg, and
1 tablespoon canola oil per cup)

1 tablespoon chia seeds

1 tablespoon ground flaxseeds

1 tablespoon natural (no sugar added)
peanut butter or almond butter

1 banana, finely chopped,
or 1 cup chopped fruit
of your choosing

MY KIDS ADORE THESE gluten-free peanut butter waffles, and I love that they are so delicious and nutritious... they have no idea how good these are for them or they might not eat them, seriously. I make these by using an easy gluten-free boxed mix, but then I tweak it to add more protein and nutrition with chia and flax. You can use the boxed mix of your choosing, but I prefer Pamela's, which I order on Amazon; it can be found at most health food stores or in the gluten-free section of your grocery store. Top the warm waffles with a fruit compote, jam, or pure maple syrup.

1. Heat a waffle iron and coat both sides with a nonstick spray.

2. Make the batter according to the directions on the box. (Note: Most important is to separate the egg white from the egg yolk, then beat the white. When the rest of the batter is mixed, use a spatula and slowly fold in the foamy egg white for added fluffiness.)

3. Stir the chia seeds, flaxseeds, and peanut butter thoroughly into the batter. Then add the fruit of your choosing (bananas are my favorite).

4. Cook in the waffle iron according to the manufacturer's directions until golden and crisp on both sides. Remove and serve.

Note: These are easy to have during the week if you freeze the waffles and then reheat or toast them for about 10 minutes.

NUTTY OVERNIGHT OATS & FRUIT

VEGETARIAN
SERVES 1

½ cup old-fashioned oats

½ cup 1% or 2% milk

½ teaspoon ground cinnamon

1 teaspoon flaxseeds

1 teaspoon chia seeds

1 teaspoon honey or agave syrup

2 tablespoons chopped fresh fruit
(peaches, strawberries, or
bananas are good choices)

1 tablespoon chopped walnuts
or almonds (optional)

THIS IS THE HEALTHY WORKHORSE of breakfasts, and a frequent go-to for me on very busy days. The night before one of these big days, I just put the oats in a mason jar, top it with the rest of the ingredients, and leave it overnight in the refrigerator. The next morning, give it a stir, and voilà . . . a balanced and delicious breakfast. If you are the type who can't think of oatmeal as a cold cereal, then heat it in the microwave (without the metal lid, of course) for about 1½ minutes, then stir and enjoy.

1. Put the oats in a mason jar, then follow with the milk, cinnamon, flaxseeds, chia, and honey. Top with the fresh fruit and walnuts, if desired.

2. Refrigerate overnight or for at least 4 hours. Serve cold, or heat in the microwave for 1½ minutes if you prefer warm oatmeal.

MANGO YOGURT MOUSSE BOWL

GLUTEN-FREE
VEGETARIAN
SERVES 4 TO 6

1 (¼-ounce) packet unflavored gelatin

2 cups pureed mango
(thawed frozen mango is fine)

3 tablespoons honey or agave nectar

½ teaspoon vanilla extract

½ cup 2% milk

½ cup plain 2% Greek yogurt

¼ cup mango slices, for topping

THIS IS SO AMAZINGLY GOOD, it's practically dessert for breakfast. I find it's a lot like a mango *lassi* milk shake from India. Make it a day or night ahead to give it time to chill and thicken. You can feel good that it has all the protein of Greek yogurt and the benefits of mango. If you don't like mango, you can substitute strawberries or another flavorful fruit.

1. In a small saucepan, dissolve the gelatin in ¼ cup cold water, then heat over medium heat until hot and clear. Remove from the heat and set aside.

2. In a blender or food processor, combine the mango puree, honey, and vanilla. Pulse to blend, then pour in the gelatin mixture, milk, and yogurt and pulse to blend smoothly.

3. Ladle the mixture into four to six small ramekins or bowls and chill, covered, overnight. The texture will be like a thick milk shake or mousse, not like Jell-O.

4. Top with the mango slices and serve.

Note: This recipe requires at least a couple of hours in the refrigerator to set.

Snacks & Smoothies

I am definitely a grazer, and so are my kids. We like to eat mini meals or healthy snacks throughout the day, then tend to eat lighter main meals. My boys are not big sweets eaters and neither am I—if I had to choose my favorite snack, it would be bread and cheese. That, however, is not something I indulge in too often, and when I do, it's with good company and a bottle of wine!

The key to smart snacks, in my opinion, is portability, so my kids and I can take them anywhere with little mess. And they need to keep me from craving the bad stuff. (You know, cookies, chips, bars, and other "fillers" that have no nutritional value and lead me down that path to diet disaster!) I'm not opposed to treating myself, but I usually try to stay on the straight and narrow by heading off those cravings with a little thought and preparation.

HUMMUS
with Veggies

GLUTEN-FREE
VEGETARIAN
MAKES ABOUT
1½ CUPS

1 (15-ounce) can chickpeas, drained and rinsed

2 tablespoons tahini

1 garlic clove, chopped

3 tablespoons fresh lemon juice

¼ cup extra-virgin olive oil, plus more for serving

Pinch of salt

Pinch of smoked paprika

½ teaspoon pine nuts, for garnish (optional)

½ teaspoon chopped fresh parsley, for garnish (optional)

HUMMUS IS AN EASY, MAKE-AHEAD SNACK to have at the ready for all those times you get a case of the munchies. I like to have celery stalks, baby carrots, peppers, and cucumbers cut up and stored in individual snack bags. And as far as hummus, it really is so easy to prepare, and I'd rather make it myself and know exactly what I'm putting into it, because too often I have seen a mix of oils or other unhealthy ingredients added to store-bought hummus.

To make it fresh, you'll need tahini, which is made from ground sesame seeds. You can find it in most grocery stores in the Middle Eastern section. Try it homemade, and you may never go back to store-bought again!

1. In a food processor, pulse the chickpeas and tahini together. Add the garlic, lemon juice, and 2 tablespoons water and process, then, with the motor running, drizzle in the olive oil until the hummus is smooth.

2. Add the salt. Serve in a bowl and sprinkle the top with the paprika. Garnish with a drizzle of olive oil, the pine nuts, and chopped parsley, if desired.

HOMEMADE COCONUT GRANOLA

VEGETARIAN
MAKES ABOUT
3½ CUPS

2 cups old-fashioned oats

½ cup unsweetened coconut flakes

¼ cup sprouted unsalted hulled
sunflower seeds

¼ cup sprouted unsalted hulled pepitas
(pumpkin seeds)

¼ cup chopped sprouted unsalted almonds

¼ cup flaxseeds

½ teaspoon ground cinnamon

½ teaspoon salt

¼ cup coconut oil, melted

¼ cup coconut syrup or pure maple syrup

1 teaspoon vanilla extract

HOW MANY TIMES HAVE YOU HEARD or read that granola isn't good for you? That's because too often, there are all kinds of unnecessary sugars or oils mixed in. But granola is so easy to make at home and really can be healthy if you keep it simple. I like to make my own granola over the weekend, and it's the perfect addition or topping for yogurt, cereal, oatmeal, or ice cream, or even by itself by the handful. I try to use sprouted nuts when possible because they are better for you. What's the difference? Basically, raw nuts have phytic acid, which is hard for the digestive system to break down completely. Sprouted nuts are essentially germinated (as if they're seeds you were going to be planting, for example), which removes some of the inhibitors and phytic acid in the nuts. Most health food stores sell sprouted nuts, but if you can't find them or they are more expensive, make your own (see sidebar).

1. Preheat the oven to 425°F.

2. In a large bowl, toss together the oats, coconut flakes, sunflower seeds, pepitas, almonds, flaxseeds, cinnamon, and salt.

3. Drizzle the coconut oil over the granola mix, using a spatula to get every bit of the oil. Drizzle in the coconut syrup and the vanilla. Using your hands, mix all together to make sure the liquids are evenly distributed.

4. Spread the granola on a baking sheet and toast for about 4 minutes, then give the granola mix a stir with a spatula (to get an even crunch), and toast until crunchy, about 4 minutes more.

5. Let it cool, then store the granola in a glass jar to preserve its freshness. Use it all week long!

Variations This is basic granola that can be tweaked and jazzed up in many ways. For example, if you want chocolate flavor, add 1 tablespoon unsweetened dark cocoa powder. Or add dried fruit, preferably unsweetened, like chopped apricots or cherries, for even more flavor.

SPROUTING NUTS

The best sprouting candidates are raw almonds, pepitas (pumpkin seeds), cashews, sunflower seeds, and walnuts. Put the raw nuts (it does not work with roasted or prepared nuts) in a glass jar with water and 1 tablespoon salt—soak different types of nuts in separate jars. Put the jars in a dark, moderately warm place (this speeds up the germination) and soak overnight or for up to 2 days. Once the nuts germinate (they will appear to sprout like a seedling, or the tops will split a bit), rinse them and place them on a cloth or paper towel to dry, then refrigerate them in an airtight container and use them within a week. To give them extra crunch and flavor, lightly roast them at 200°F for about 10 minutes—or make my granola already!

FROZEN BANANAS with Nutella & Nuts

GLUTEN-FREE
VEGETARIAN
SERVES 4

4 ripe medium bananas (not frozen)

4 to 6 tablespoons Nutella

¼ cup chopped unsalted pistachios, peanuts, or almonds

ONE OF THE EASIEST SNACKS and a kid favorite! This is a pick-me-up I give my kids before a soccer game or even instead of dessert. Before a long run or on training runs for marathons, this was also my go-to because it's the perfect fuel with its combination of carbs, protein, and healthy fats. Give me anything that's loaded with nuts, bananas, and chocolate, and I'm in heaven. (See page 47 for my favorite banana and peanut butter combo!)

1. Peel and then slice the bananas in half lengthwise. Spread a generous tablespoon of the Nutella on one half. Sprinkle with the chopped nuts. Put the other half of the banana on top. If it won't stick well, add a little Nutella on that side too. Repeat with the remaining bananas.

2. Individually wrap each banana in plastic wrap and store in a resealable plastic bag in the freezer. Freeze them overnight or for up to a few days. They're best if enjoyed within the week.

COCOA-NUTTY POWER BALLS

VEGETARIAN
MAKES 15 TO 20

½ cup roasted unsalted cashews

½ cup hulled pepitas (pumpkin seeds)

10 pitted dates

½ cup Ezekiel 4:9 Almond Sprouted Whole-Grain Cereal or Grape-Nuts

½ cup old-fashioned oats

½ cup sweetened shredded coconut

1 tablespoon coconut manna or raw coconut butter

2 tablespoons unsweetened cocoa powder

2 large egg whites

1 tablespoon agave nectar, pure maple syrup, or honey

THESE SNACKS ARE A REALLY GOOD SUBSTITUTE for those great-sounding but not-great-for-you energy bars. Commercial bars are often loaded with processed ingredients, whereas this recipe is full of healthy carbs and proteins like oats and an Ezekiel cereal made from legumes and almonds. Sweetened with dates, these are further enriched with unsweetened cocoa and cinnamon, both powerful antioxidants. And most important to my family, Cocoa-Nutty Power Balls taste much better than a granola bar—just ask my youngest, Luke, who happily grabs a couple of these on his way to soccer practice.

---

1. Preheat the oven to 350°F.

2. In food processor, combine the cashews, pepitas, and dates and process until still a bit chunky. Add the cereal and pulse a few times.

3. In a large bowl, mix together the oats, sweetened coconut, coconut manna, cocoa powder, and egg whites. Stir in the nut blend and mix all together. Add the agave and stir to combine.

4. Roll the mixture into balls, about 1 tablespoon each, and bake on a large baking sheet for about 10 minutes, turning the balls over halfway through. Set on a wire rack to cool. These can be stored in an airtight container at room temperature for up to a week or frozen for up to a month.

EVERYDAY GREEN SMOOTHIE

GLUTEN-FREE
VEGETARIAN
SERVES 1

½ cup chopped frozen mango chunks

¼ cup coconut water

2 or 3 ice cubes

½ large apple, cored and chopped

1 cup baby kale or spinach

½ medium cucumber, unpeeled
and well washed if the skin
is thin and pristine

Juice of 1 lemon

1 tablespoon chopped fresh mint

1 teaspoon chia seeds

MY "BREAKFAST OF CHAMPIONS," this super-packed green smoothie doesn't look appetizing, but it is the way I start my day most every weekday morning. It's not always green, as I sometimes add berries or other fruits, but the base ingredient is spinach or kale. It's part of my preshow routine because I can't stomach a big breakfast at four A.M. This and a snack of almond butter toast get me through most of the show. It gives me the energy boost I need first thing, and it starts my day with a big dose of superfoods, which ensure that I'm getting all the nutrients I need regardless of what challenges arise. Just be sure you have a good blender that can truly liquefy most vegetables and ice.

1. In a powerful blender, combine the mango, ½ cup water, the coconut water, and ice and blend until smooth. Add the apple, kale, cucumber, lemon, mint, and chia seeds and blend again until smooth.

2. Pour into a glass container or portable bottle. Refrigerate until you are ready to enjoy.

Note: For extra creaminess, you can add ¼ cup avocado—optional, of course.

HEART-HEALTHY RED SMOOTHIE

GLUTEN-FREE
VEGETARIAN
SERVES 1

1 cup flax milk or almond milk

1 frozen banana, chopped

2 or 3 ice cubes

2 cups mixed frozen berries

½ cup frozen cherries

2 teaspoons chia seeds

1 tablespoon honey
or agave nectar (optional)

THIS IS A VARIATION ON MY MORNING SMOOTHIE, and to be honest, it tastes more like a delicious dessert. I like to use frozen raspberries, strawberries, blueberries, cherries, and bananas. One tip: When my bananas start to get overripe, I simply peel them, cut them up, and freeze them in resealable plastic bags so I always have them frozen and ready to go for my smoothies. If you want a milk shake consistency, it's best to enjoy this smoothie right away, but you can always give it a vigorous shake and enjoy later in the day.

1. In a powerful blender, combine the flax milk, banana, and ice and blend until smooth. Add the berries, cherries, chia seeds, and honey (if using) and blend again until smooth.

2. Pour into a glass container or portable bottle. Refrigerate until you are ready to enjoy.

3-MINUTE PEANUT BUTTER & BANANA PROTEIN SHAKE

GLUTEN-FREE
VEGETARIAN
SERVES 1

½ cup flax milk or almond milk

1 frozen banana, chopped

4 ice cubes

1 tablespoon unsweetened or natural peanut butter

1 tablespoon vanilla or plain whey protein

1 tablespoon ground flaxseeds

1 tablespoon honey or agave nectar (optional)

ONE OF MY FAVORITE COMBINATIONS, bananas and peanut butter! This is so deliciously filling while also giving you all the nutrients you need to keep you going all morning long (or if you need a burst of energy and recovery after a workout). I like to add a little whey protein and flax meal to give me just a little more bang, then I'm usually good until lunch.

1. In a powerful blender, combine the flax milk, ¼ cup water, the banana, and ice cubes and blend until smooth. Add the peanut butter, whey protein, flaxseeds, and honey (if using) and blend again until smooth.

2. Drink right away, preferably, or refrigerate and drink within 4 hours.

Variation For your chocolate fix, add 1 tablespoon unsweetened cocoa powder and 1 tablespoon agave nectar or honey, if desired, along with all the rest and enjoy as much as a banana split!

Lunch on the Go

Many of us lead our lives constantly on the go, so eating healthy goes quickly by the wayside. With my jam-packed schedule of working for both *TODAY* and *Access Hollywood*, I have had a hard time figuring out when and what to eat. I think the stress-free way is to plan ahead–this is a big theme in my life. The night before, pack a lunch to go that is well balanced and healthy and includes plenty of snacks. And if I'm really forward-thinking, I plan for the week over the weekend, making a rotisserie chicken, pasta sauce, extra quinoa or farro, and cutting up veggies to give myself plenty of options throughout the week for salads and meals that the whole family will love. Here are a few of those quickies for lunch that are perfect for that fast-paced, multitasking, busy somebody you no doubt are!

ASIAN FARRO CHICKEN SALAD

SERVES 4

DRESSING

¼ cup vegetable oil or canola oil

3 tablespoons fresh lime juice

2 tablespoons low-sodium soy sauce

2 tablespoons rice vinegar

1 tablespoon honey

Pinch of salt

Pinch of freshly ground black pepper

Pinch of red pepper flakes (optional)

SALAD

1 carrot, shredded

½ red bell pepper, cut into thin strips

½ cup chopped seeded cucumber

½ cup thawed and shelled frozen edamame

¼ cup finely chopped red onion

1 cup mixed salad greens

1 cup shredded Chinese (napa) cabbage

2 cups chopped cooked or grilled chicken (use leftover rotisserie chicken or chicken breast)

2 cups cooked farro (cooked according to package directions, or cooked quinoa as a gluten-free option)

¼ cup chopped peanuts

¼ chopped fresh cilantro

IS FARRO THE NEXT QUINOA? What you may not know about this ancient grain is that it's just as powerful as that well-known superfood. It's packed with protein and fiber, like quinoa, but has more calcium and slightly more complex carbs, too. Also, contrary to what some people think, it is not a pasta like orzo—it is a grain, more like brown rice, though it is not gluten-free.

Farro has been a staple in Italy for centuries, but is gaining popularity quickly in the U.S., perhaps because, like quinoa, it is so versatile. It can be mixed with just about anything for breakfast, lunch, and/or dinner. Try cooking it like a risotto—or sweeten it up with honey or maple syrup, granola, and fruit and it's a breakfast cereal. Plus, it's a perfect grain base in a minestrone or hearty soup or stew.

1. **Make the dressing:** In a mason jar, combine the vegetable oil, lime juice, soy sauce, vinegar, 2 tablespoons water, the honey, salt, black pepper, and red pepper flakes (if using). Give it a good shake and use only as much dressing as you need per serving.

2. **Make the salad:** In a bowl, combine the carrot, bell pepper, cucumber, edamame, and red onion.

3. When you're preparing this salad for a to-go lunch, pack it in a large plastic bowl with a lid. Layer the salad greens, then cabbage, then chicken, then farro (or quinoa). Top with the vegetable mixture. Sprinkle with the peanuts and cilantro. If serving this to a larger group, the chicken and farro can be served warm on a bed of the cold vegetables, then drizzled with the dressing.

CHICKEN PEANUT SATAY SALAD

SERVES 4

DRESSING

3 tablespoons fresh lime juice

3 tablespoons vegetable oil or canola oil

2 tablespoons natural creamy peanut butter

2 tablespoons rice vinegar

1 tablespoon low-sodium soy sauce

1 teaspoon honey or sugar

SALAD

1 head romaine lettuce, chopped, or 4 cups mixed salad greens

2 cups chopped or shredded cooked chicken (use leftover rotisserie or grilled chicken)

1 cup chopped snow peas

1 large cucumber, peeled, seeded and cut into small cubes

1 large red bell pepper, halved lengthwise and thinly sliced

½ cup shredded carrot

2 green onions, thinly sliced

¼ cup chopped fresh cilantro

¼ cup unsalted sliced almonds

Crispy Rice Noodles (recipe follows), for garnish (optional)

SIMILAR TO THE ASIAN FARRO CHICKEN SALAD (page 50), we are using a rotisserie chicken or precooked grilled chicken breast here, making this a quick-assembly and low-hassle lunch or light dinner. Make it and it will be a family favorite for sure. I'm a fan of the peanut satay dressing, which is lighter than the typically heavy Thai sauce, so no need to feel guilty. My kids love the crispy rice noodles added to the salad, but if you want to go lighter, just stick to the salad ingredients you like and top with the chicken, salad dressing, and a sprinkle of unsalted sliced almonds.

---

1. **Make the dressing:** In a glass jar, combine the lime juice, vegetable oil, peanut butter, 2 tablespoons water, the vinegar, soy sauce, and honey. Shake thoroughly. Set aside.

2. **Make the salad:** In a large serving bowl, toss the lettuce, chicken, snow peas, cucumber, bell pepper, carrot, and green onion. Top with the cilantro and sliced almonds. Crumble in the crispy rice noodles, if desired, or serve the salad on top of a bed of the crispy rice noodles.

3. Drizzle with the dressing only upon serving.

CRISPY RICE NOODLES

SERVES 4

2 cups peanut oil or vegetable oil

1 (8-ounce) package rice vermicelli noodles

Salt

1. Line a plate with paper towels. In a large deep skillet or wok, heat the peanut oil over medium-high heat.

2. When the oil is very hot (drop in a noodle to see if it sizzles), slide in the rice noodles. They will puff up and cook within a few seconds, so don't let them burn. Remove the crispy noodles from the oil and drain them on the paper towel–lined plate. Season lightly with salt.

HEALTHY CHICKEN COBB SALAD

with Avocado-Yogurt Vinaigrette

GLUTEN-FREE
SERVES 4

DRESSING

1 ripe avocado, pitted and peeled

½ cup plain Greek yogurt

¼ cup extra-virgin olive oil

¼ cup chopped fresh cilantro

Juice of 1 lime

1 tablespoon chopped fresh parsley

Salt

SALAD

1 head romaine lettuce, chopped

2 cups firmly packed baby spinach leaves, chopped

2 cups chopped cooked chicken (use leftover rotisserie or grilled chicken)

1 cup chopped tomatoes

1 cup chopped canned chickpeas (drain and rinse before chopping)

½ cup finely chopped red onion

½ cup chopped peeled cucumber

½ cup diced Swiss, feta, or shredded mozzarella cheese

2 large eggs, hard-boiled and chopped

THIS IS NOT YOUR ORDINARY CHOPPED COBB SALAD; what truly makes it spectacular is the Avocado-Yogurt Vinaigrette. My husband loves this dressing on just about anything, and the best part about it is that it's heart-healthy, with all the wonderful omega fats and calcium and protein from the Greek yogurt. You will want to drink the dressing on its own, it's that delicious. No bacon here to keep it healthy, but it's up to you. If you need it, then by all means, go for it.

1. **Make the dressing:** In a blender, combine the avocado, yogurt, ½ cup water, the olive oil, cilantro, lime juice, and parsley. Blend until smooth, adding up to ½ cup more water, a little at a time, until the desired consistency is reached. Season with salt.

2. **Make the salad:** In a large serving bowl or in individual salad bowls, layer the romaine and baby spinach on the bottom. Arrange the chicken, tomatoes, chickpeas, red onion, cucumbers, cheese, and chopped egg in an attractive pattern on top of the greens—e.g., radiating out or in concentric circles.

3. When ready to serve, drizzle the salad with the dressing.

SOBA NOODLE & VEGETABLE SALAD

VEGETARIAN
SERVES 4 TO 6

1 (10-ounce) box or bag soba noodles

1 cup chopped broccoli florets

2 tablespoons extra-virgin olive oil

1 cup thinly sliced shiitake mushrooms

1 garlic clove, minced

1 red bell pepper, cut into small strips

1 cup shredded carrots

1 cup thawed and shelled frozen edamame

Salt and freshly ground black pepper

DRESSING

5 tablespoons rice vinegar

1 tablespoon toasted sesame oil

1 tablespoon extra-virgin olive oil

1 tablespoon low-sodium soy sauce

1 tablespoon agave nectar

1 tablespoon fresh lime juice

½ teaspoon grated fresh ginger

2 green onions, thinly sliced

1 tablespoon black sesame seeds, for topping

YOU CAN CALL SOBA THE HEALTHIER PASTA because it is made from buckwheat and wheat flour, which lends the noodles an earthier or nutty taste. It cooks just as easily as regular pasta and works for lunch or dinner. Plus, they're delicious hot or cold, so perfect for a portable meal.

I like this soba salad paired with a wide assortment of seasonal veggies—and feel free to top it with a lean protein like tofu, chicken, shrimp, or salmon.

1. Bring a large pot of salted water to a boil, add the soba noodles, and cook according to the instructions on the package. Don't let the noodles get too soft; you want them a little al dente. When done, drain and set the noodles aside in a large bowl.

2. Fill a large bowl with ice and water. In a vegetable steamer or a steamer basket in a pot, bring some water to a boil. Steam the broccoli until tender but still very green, 2 to 3 minutes. Remove the steamed broccoli and plunge it quickly into the ice water for about 30 seconds, to keep it green and crunchy. Set aside.

3. In a large skillet, heat the olive oil over medium heat. Add the mushrooms and garlic and cook, stirring, for 1 minute. Add the bell pepper, carrots, and edamame and cook, stirring continuously, until they're coated in the garlic oil and softened a bit, about 1 minute. Season with salt and black pepper.

4. **Make the dressing:** In a glass bowl, whisk together the vinegar, sesame oil, olive oil, soy sauce, agave, lime juice, and ginger.

5. Toss all the vegetables and the green onions with the soba noodles and drizzle liberally with the dressing, letting it soak into the noodles. Sprinkle the sesame seeds in and toss the noodles again, to make sure the dressing is spread evenly.

SUPERFOOD SALMON QUINOA SALAD

SERVES 2 TO 4

SALMON IS ONE OF MY FAVORITE FOODS, and it is so healthy. Only problem: When I broil it or bake it, it stinks up the whole house, and my husband can't stand the smell. So poaching the salmon in seasoned liquid is the answer. Poaching preserves the flavor while allowing you to cook the fish in 15 to 20 minutes flat.

SALMON

½ cup dry white wine, or ⅓ cup fresh lemon juice

¼ cup chopped shallots

1 tablespoon drained capers (optional)

2 sprigs fresh dill, or 1 teaspoon dried

2 sprigs fresh parsley

Salt and freshly ground black pepper

1 pound skin-on salmon fillet(s)

1 tablespoon unsalted butter

QUINOA SALAD

2 cups cooked quinoa (prepared according to the package instructions)

2 cups chopped baby kale

1 cucumber, chopped

½ cup chopped sun-dried tomatoes in oil

½ cup crumbled feta cheese

¼ cup chopped red onion

2 tablespoons chopped fresh parsley

1 tablespoon minced fresh oregano, or 1 teaspoon dried

1 tablespoon minced fresh mint leaves

3 tablespoons extra-virgin olive oil

3 tablespoons fresh lemon juice

Salt and freshly ground black pepper

1. **Make the salmon:** In a medium skillet, combine the wine, ⅓ cup water, the shallots, capers, dill, and parsley and bring to a boil over medium-high heat.

2. Season the salmon with salt and pepper and put on top of the herbs in the skillet with the skin-side down. Top with the butter.

3. Lower the heat to medium and cook, covered, for about 8 minutes for medium, or to your preference. Remove from the skillet with some of the capers and dill. Cut into two or four pieces and set aside.

4. **Make the quinoa salad:** In a large bowl, toss the quinoa, kale, cucumber, sun-dried tomatoes, feta, red onion, parsley, oregano, and mint. In a small bowl, whisk together the olive oil and lemon juice. Dress the salad, then season with salt and pepper.

5. To serve, plate the salad first, then top with the salmon. The salmon can be served at any temperature.

HEALTHY SWEET POTATO SALAD

GLUTEN-FREE
VEGETARIAN
SERVES 6

4 large sweet potatoes (2½ to 3 pounds total), peeled and cut into 1-inch cubes

¼ cup plus 2 to 3 tablespoons extra-virgin olive oil

1 cup thinly sliced celery (about 3 stalks)

½ small red onion, thinly sliced

½ cup thawed and shelled frozen edamame

2 tablespoons fresh lemon juice

1 tablespoon Dijon mustard

Salt and freshly ground black pepper

¼ cup chopped fresh parsley

1 tablespoon minced fresh chives

Toasted pepitas (pumpkin seeds; see Tip), for garnish (optional)

Tip: To toast pumpkin seeds, preheat the oven to 375°F. Toss the seeds lightly with olive oil, then spread them out on a rimmed baking sheet. Cook until crispy and light brown, 6 to 8 minutes, stirring them halfway through.

THIS IS A NEW VARIATION on the old picnic potato salad of yore . . . the (unhealthy) summertime staple that we all find so good. Sweet potatoes are a much healthier alternative to those white potatoes, and I think much tastier, so I came up with a better-for-you version. Edamame and fresh herbs make it even yummier, while packing in lots of health benefits. For a heartier meal, I top it with grilled chicken, which I make alongside the salad in preparation for weekday lunches.

1. Preheat the oven to 400°F.

2. Put the cubed potatoes on a large baking sheet (or two, if you can't get them all on in a single layer). Drizzle the potatoes with 2 to 3 tablespoons of the olive oil, ensuring all the cubes are coated. Spread the potatoes out in a single layer. Roast for 25 to 30 minutes, until the potatoes are tender and browned, stirring them halfway through. Set aside.

3. In a large bowl, stir together the celery, red onion, and edamame. Stir the potatoes into the onion mixture and set aside.

4. In a small bowl, whisk together the remaining ¼ cup olive oil, lemon juice, and mustard. Drizzle the vinaigrette over the potatoes and toss gently. Season with salt and pepper. Stir in the parsley and chives and serve immediately, or cover and refrigerate, adding the parsley and chives just before serving so that the herbs remain crisp and fresh, not wilted. Sprinkle with pepitas, if you like added crunch.

CAULIFLOWER-CRUST QUICHE
with Cheese, Broccoli & Mushrooms

GLUTEN-FREE
VEGETARIAN
SERVES 6 TO 8

CAULIFLOWER CRUST
1 head cauliflower

Nonstick cooking spray

1 large egg

½ cup freshly grated Parmesan cheese

¼ cup shredded mozzarella cheese

1 teaspoon fresh thyme or ½ teaspoon dried thyme

¼ teaspoon garlic powder

Pinch of salt

FILLING
6 large eggs

½ cup heavy cream

½ cup grated Gruyère or cheddar cheese (Gruyère is creamier but a bit sharper)

¼ cup freshly grated Parmesan cheese

Pinch of salt

Pinch of freshly ground black pepper

Pinch of cayenne pepper

Pinch of ground nutmeg

1 cup chopped broccoli florets

¾ cup thinly sliced white mushrooms

½ cup finely diced yellow onion

6 slices cooked bacon, crumbled, or ½ cup chopped ham (optional)

CAULIFLOWER DOESN'T GET AS MUCH RESPECT AS IT DESERVES, but I like using it in so many recipes like this one, or as a Paleo cauliflower rice, or even grilled like a steak. It truly is so versatile, and here it makes a perfect light crust for a quiche. The best part is, it's low-carb and gluten-free and a great way to sneak veggies into your kids! Just make sure you squeeze out as much of the water from the grated cauliflower as you can to try to keep the crust from being too soggy. Cheesecloth is a good way to do this, then let it dry for about an hour. Next, load in the filling and bake!

1. **Make the cauliflower crust:** Cut the cauliflower into large chunks, then either grate each by hand to rice the cauliflower or pulse in a food processor until a granulated texture is achieved.

2. Microwave the cauliflower in a covered dish until cooked, about 8 minutes, then uncover and allow it cool for several minutes. When it's cool enough to handle, place the cauliflower in a double layer of cheesecloth or a clean dishtowel and squeeze out as much liquid as you can. Set aside in an uncovered bowl to dry for 1 hour.

3. Preheat the oven to 425°F. Line the bottom of an 8- to 10-inch pie plate with a piece of parchment paper cut to fit. Spray the sides of the pie plate and the parchment lightly with nonstick spray.

4. In a large glass bowl, whisk together the egg, Parmesan, mozzarella, thyme, garlic powder, and salt. Stir in the cauliflower.

recipe continues

Note: You'll want the creaminess of heavy cream; don't substitute milk.

5. Evenly spread and press the cauliflower crust "dough" onto the bottom and up the sides of the pie plate, poking it in a few places toward the middle with a fork to help prevent bubbling (you may need to do this once or twice while it bakes as well, if it starts to puff up in the middle).

6. Bake the crust until golden and set, 15 to 20 minutes. Set aside. Lower the oven temperature to 350°F.

7. **Make the filling:** In a large bowl, whisk together the eggs, cream, Gruyère, Parmesan, salt, black pepper, cayenne, and nutmeg. Stir in the broccoli, mushrooms, and onion. Stir in the bacon, if desired.

8. Pour the egg-vegetable mixture into the cauliflower crust. Bake until the egg is set in the middle, 25 to 30 minutes. Slice into wedges and enjoy.

TOFU VEGGIE QUINOA BOWL

VEGETARIAN
SERVES 8 TO 10

2 (12- to 14-ounce) packages
or bricks firm tofu, drained

3 tablespoons fresh orange juice

2 tablespoons low-sodium soy sauce

2 tablespoons toasted sesame oil

2 garlic cloves, minced

½ cup chopped yellow onion

16 ounces white mushrooms or shiitake
mushrooms, washed and thinly sliced

2 cups chopped broccoli florets

1 cup sliced carrots (cut into coins)

1 red bell pepper, diced

1½ cups cooked quinoa (prepared
according to the package instructions)

2 green onions, thinly sliced

Salt and freshly ground black pepper

I HAVE MADE THIS DISH MANY TIMES for my vegetarian friends, and have taken it to many barbecues and potlucks. It's a people-pleaser while also being good for you. You can eat it at any temperature, making it easy to bring along and serve up in any setting, and it's still delicious two days later as a to-go lunch. If you don't like tofu, replace it with the protein of your choosing. Serve it as is or add a hummus dip (see page 36) on the side. One thing I like to do is water down plain hummus a little so it creates more of a creamy tahini sauce, then drizzle it on top.

1. Pat the tofu well with paper towels to dry it off. Cut it into 1-inch cubes.

2. In a wok or large skillet, stir together the orange juice, soy sauce, sesame oil, and garlic. Add the cubed tofu and yellow onion and cook over medium heat, stirring frequently, until they have absorbed the flavors, about 3 minutes, then transfer to a plate and set aside.

3. In the same wok or skillet, stir together the mushrooms, broccoli, carrots and bell pepper. Cook over medium-high heat, stirring constantly, until the broccoli is cooked crisp-tender or al dente, 3 to 4 minutes.

4. Add the quinoa, tofu-onion mixture, and green onions, tossing to stir it all up. Season with salt and black pepper.

Party Appetizers

Entertaining at our house is never formal, and it's always a family affair. We keep it low-key, and no matter how hard I try to shuffle guests into the living room or dining room, the kitchen is always the center of the action. Accordingly, I like to serve casual, approachable food using simple ingredients, and I'll never make something that requires me to stay in the kitchen the entire time—that's not entertaining! Neighbors, friends, or family come over for a barbecue every other weekend, when we don't have soccer games to attend, and we do make-your-own pizzas on the grill or something equally unfussy. Kids are always all around us, everywhere, and it's usually chaos.

For appetizers I take my cues from my time growing up in Madrid, Spain—small tapas-like things that are very flavorful but not too filling. My kids are always on the move at our parties, so I like to have finger foods that are grab-and-go.

CHICKEN EMPANADAS

12 (6-inch) frozen empanada shells or Homemade Empanada Shells (recipe follows)

2 tablespoons extra-virgin olive oil

1½ pounds chicken breasts

½ yellow onion, diced

2 garlic cloves, minced

2 cups chicken broth

¼ cup tomato paste

2 teaspoons red wine vinegar

2 teaspoons ground cumin

2 teaspoons chili powder, plus more if needed

1 teaspoon dried oregano

Tabasco sauce, for extra kick (optional)

Salt and freshly ground black pepper

1½ cups diced white potatoes (¼-inch cubes)

½ cup diced pimiento-stuffed Manzanilla olives

½ cup dark raisins (optional)

All-purpose flour, for dusting

1 large egg, lightly beaten with 1 teaspoon water in a small bowl

MAKING EMPANADAS always reminds me of my mom because this is her go-to recipe for entertaining. At any family gathering, holiday, or visit with friends, these empanadas are the center of attention and are usually gone within minutes of serving. My *abuelita*, my grandmother from Puerto Rico, taught my mom how to make them, who then taught my sisters and me, and so it goes. It's a recipe passed down over generations with love and a desire to preserve one small part of our cultural heritage, wherever we end up living. Typically they are filled with ground beef and have raisins and potatoes— I find the combo of sweet and savory to be part of their appeal, but the raisins are optional, if you prefer not to use them. Traditional empanadas are fried, but baking them saves some fat and calories, and they're just as good with the addition of a nice golden sheen.

If you have a grocery store with a robust Spanish section, it will be easy to find the frozen empanada shells, but if you can't buy them, don't let that keep you from trying to make them. I've included my own dough recipe and it's easier than you think.

1. If you're using frozen empanada shells, thaw them to room temperature.

2. In a large skillet, heat the olive oil over medium heat, then place the chicken breasts in the pan. Brown and cook until the juices in the chicken run clear, 5 to 6 minutes on each side.

recipe continues

Remove the chicken from the pan and allow to cool. Using two forks, shred the chicken.

3. In the same pan, cook the onion and garlic over medium heat, stirring, until the onion is softened, 2 to 3 minutes.

4. Add the shredded chicken, broth, tomato paste, and vinegar and stir. Season with the cumin, chili powder, oregano, and a dash or two of Tabasco, if desired. Taste and season with salt and pepper and more chili powder, if need be.

5. Stir in the potatoes, olives, and raisins (if using). Reduce the heat to low, cover, and simmer until the chicken becomes very tender and pulls apart even more easily, about 15 minutes.

6. Preheat the oven to 350°F. Line a large baking sheet with parchment paper and sprinkle a dash of flour on the surface.

7. Assemble the empanadas on the prepared baking sheet. Put 2 tablespoons of the filling in the middle of a shell. Use your index finger to wipe the beaten egg on the outer edge of the shell. Fold the shell over and seal the edges using a fork. Repeat with the remaining shells.

8. Brush the tops with the egg wash. On a clean baking sheet, bake the empanadas for about 20 minutes, or until the shells are nice and golden.

Variations

Once you get the hang of it, you can try loads of variations. I make beef, veggie, and cheese empanadas, which my kids really like.

FOR BEEF EMPANADAS: Substitute 1½ pounds lean ground sirloin for the chicken breasts and use beef broth in place of the chicken broth.

FOR CHEESY FRIED EMPANADAS: These are the mozzarella sticks of the Latin world. I recommend frying them because this way you get the melted cheese center in a flaky golden empanada crust. They were always my favorite when my grandmother would make them for us. Now my kids also love the cheese empanadas best because they are like a fluffy fried quesadilla.

Fill a large skillet one-quarter of the way with vegetable oil and heat over medium heat until a drop of flour or piece of dough sizzles when it hits the oil. Stuff your empanada shells with about 2 tablespoons each of grated manchego or mozzarella cheese. Seal them with the egg wash as directed and use a fork to press the seams together with indentations. Fry them in batches, flipping them from one side to the other when golden. Remove and drain on a plate lined with paper towels. Serve very hot, with a side of salsa or tomato sauce for dipping.

FOR SPINACH, MUSHROOM & MANCHEGO CHEESE EMPANADAS: For my vegetarian friends, I usually whip up a batch of these delicious empanadas alongside my meat or chicken empanadas, so there's always something for everyone.

In a skillet, heat 2 tablespoons olive oil over medium heat. Add about 1 cup thinly sliced white mushrooms and ½ cup finely chopped yellow onion and cook, stirring, until the onions start to become translucent, about 5 minutes. Stir in 1 pound baby spinach and cook until it is wilted but still green, just a few minutes. Add ¼ cup vegetable broth, and season with salt and pepper. Separately, grate about 1 cup manchego cheese. Fill the empanada shells with the spinach and mushroom mixture, then add about 2 tablespoons of the cheese. Fold and seal the empanadas as directed, then either fry them or bake them as directed above. (Makes 8 to 10 empanadas.)

HOMEMADE EMPANADA SHELLS

MAKES ABOUT 12 SHELLS

⅓ cup ice water

1 large egg

1 tablespoon distilled white vinegar

2 cups all-purpose flour,
plus more for dusting

¾ teaspoon salt

½ cup (1 stick) very cold unsalted
butter, cut into cubes

1. In a bowl, beat the ice water, egg, and vinegar with a fork. (The ice water and vinegar ensure that the dough stays flaky.)

2. In a large bowl, whisk together the flour and salt, then cut the cold butter into the mixture using two knives or with your fingers.

3. Make a well in the flour mixture and pour in the egg mixture. Stir with a fork until the flour is incorporated. Put the dough on a floured surface and knead until the dough is smooth. Form the dough into a ball, then a flattened disc. Wrap it in plastic wrap and refrigerate for at least 1 hour, but not more than 24 hours. (Or you can freeze the dough at this stage for later use.)

4. On a floured surface, roll the dough out to about ⅛ inch thick, then cut it into 6-inch rounds. Proceed to fill and bake as directed.

ROSEMARY-PARMESAN BREADSTICKS

VEGETARIAN
MAKES 24

1 teaspoon sugar

2½ teaspoons active dry yeast

2¼ cups plus 2 tablespoons all-purpose flour, plus more as needed

½ cup plus 2 tablespoons freshly grated Parmesan cheese

2 tablespoons extra-virgin olive oil, plus more for brushing

2 teaspoons minced fresh rosemary

1 teaspoon sea salt

1 tablespoon unsalted butter, for greasing

1 tablespoon coarse sea salt (optional)

THESE BREADSTICKS ARE CRISPY AND DELICIOUS. Stand them up in a vase lined with a decorative dishtowel or place in a breadbasket in the center of the table.

1. Put 1 cup warm water in a large bowl, stir in the sugar, and sprinkle the yeast over the top. Wait until it foams, 3 to 5 minutes.

2. Using a hand mixer, mix in 1 cup of the flour, ½ cup of the Parmesan, the olive oil, rosemary, and salt. Beat for about 5 minutes, then add 1 cup more flour, until it makes a soft dough. Then either knead by hand or in the bowl of a stand mixer using the dough hook to incorporate another ¼ cup of the flour. Kneading will take about 10 minutes until you get the desired texture, like a pizza dough. It should be smooth and springy, not sticky. Add more flour by the tablespoon as needed to get the desired consistency.

3. On a floured baking mat or counter, form the dough into a rectangle about the size of a brick. Brush the dough with olive oil and cover with plastic wrap. Set it aside at room temperature to rise for about 1 hour.

4. Preheat the oven to 350°F. Line two baking sheets with parchment paper and grease the parchment with the butter.

recipe continues

5. If needed (if the dough is sticking to the surface), sprinkle the dough with the remaining 2 tablespoons flour. Divide the dough into 6 sections, then divide the dough two more times to make about 24 pieces total. Roll each piece and stretch them out into thin 10- to 12-inch-long strips. (The thinner the strip, the crunchier the breadstick will be.)

6. Place the dough strips on the prepared baking sheets, spacing them ½ inch apart. Brush with olive oil and sprinkle lightly with the remaining 2 tablespoons Parmesan or a bit of coarse sea salt, if desired.

7. Bake until golden brown, 8 to 10 minutes on each side. Let cool and serve.

Variations If you prefer, substitute other herbs for the rosemary and Parmesan, use smoked paprika, or try making "everything bagel" sticks with a mixture of sesame, poppy seed, dried garlic, and dried onion sprinkled on top. For a sweet stick, add cinnamon and sugar.

[SPANISH TAPAS PLATTER]

SPANISH TAPAS PLATTER:
Chicken Croquettes, Olives, Manchego, Jamón Serrano & Jam

SERVES 8

1 pound 6-month aged manchego cheese, sliced

½ pound thinly sliced jamón Serrano

1½ cups olives (black, Manzanilla, or stuffed with anchovy, garlic, or almond)

½ cup fig jam

Chicken Croquettes (recipe follows)

Baguette or country bread, sliced

AN ODE TO SPAIN, this is a traditional spread of small bites, perfect with a cocktail in hand. (In fact, *tapa* means "cover" or "lid," and it's claimed that tapas started out as a humble hunk of bread used as a drink cover in Spanish bars.) From sautéed garlic shrimp to spicy tomato meatballs, there are as many types of little tapas dishes as the day is long. Easy additions to this tapas platter might be a sprinkle of dried fruits like apricots and cherries on the side along with fresh cut greenery, blanched almonds, sautéed slices of chorizo, small cubes of my Tortilla Española (page 240), or add my Empanadas (page 66) fresh out of the oven and sliced in half. If you can't find slices of dry-cured jamón Serrano, prosciutto can be substituted. Fig jam works wonderfully with the cheese and ham, but other options include onion, pepper, apricot, or even orange marmalade.

On an extra-large cheese tray, platter, or butcher block, fan out slices of the manchego along with gently folded slices of charcuterie, in this case jamón Serrano. In the center, put a small bowl of the mixed olives and the fig jam along with a serving spoon or knife. Along the other side, arrange the croquettes (piping hot out of the oven!) and thin slices of the baguette.

CHICKEN CROQUETTES

5 tablespoons unsalted butter

½ cup plus 2 tablespoons all-purpose flour

½ cup plus 2 tablespoons whole milk

½ cup chicken broth

¼ cup minced yellow onion

¼ cup minced celery

3 cups minced cooked chicken
(about 1¼ pounds uncooked)

1 teaspoon minced fresh parsley

½ teaspoon fresh thyme leaves

Pinch of celery seeds (optional)

Dash of cayenne pepper

Pinch of salt

Pinch of freshly ground black pepper

2 large eggs

1 cup Italian seasoned dry bread crumbs

Vegetable oil, for frying

CROQUETTES ARE ONE OF MY FAVORITE APPETIZERS because they are so easy to make and everyone loves how the warm, crunchy-coated pieces just melt in your mouth. In Spain, croquettes come in many flavors: jamón Serrano, chicken, fish, you name it—they're a national delicacy. They're also very popular in Brazil, so I had to give you my take on this savory classic given my love of both countries. The best part about this recipe is that it uses up your leftover chicken or rotisserie chicken. My mom even makes croquettes with leftover Thanksgiving turkey, stuffing, and/or mashed potatoes.

1. In a medium saucepan, melt 4 tablespoons of the butter, then whisk in ½ cup of the flour. Whisk in ½ cup of the milk and the broth. Cook, whisking continuously, to thicken, 4 to 6 minutes, then remove from the heat and let cool for 10 minutes.

2. In a skillet, melt the remaining 1 tablespoon butter over medium heat. Add the onion and celery and cook, stirring, until lightly softened, about 2 minutes.

3. In a large bowl, mix the cooked chicken, onion-celery mixture, parsley, thyme, celery seeds (if using), and cayenne. Season with the salt and black pepper. Stir in the roux to make the croquette paste. Divide and form into about 16 sausage-like rolls, about 2½ by 1 inches; they will be a bit wet.

4. In a shallow bowl, whisk the eggs with the remaining 2 tablespoons milk. In a separate shallow bowl, mix the bread crumbs

recipe continues

and remaining 2 tablespoons flour. Dredge the croquettes first in the egg and then roll in the bread crumb mixture. Arrange the croquettes on a baking sheet and refrigerate for up to 2 hours.

5. Preheat the oven to 250°F. Line a baking sheet with parchment paper.

6. In a deep skillet, heat about ½ inch of vegetable oil to 350°F—you'll know it's ready when you can drop in a bit of flour and it sizzles. Fry the croquettes in batches, rotating them on all sides until they are golden brown, 4 to 6 minutes total. As you go, transfer the fried croquettes to the prepared sheet pan and keep warm in the oven until all batches are done. Serve right away.

BAKED FIG & RICOTTA

GLUTEN-FREE
VEGETARIAN
MAKES 8 TO 10 STUFFED FIGS

½ cup fresh ricotta cheese

1 tablespoon fresh lemon juice

1½ teaspoons fresh thyme leaves

8 to 10 fresh purple or green figs

2 tablespoons balsamic vinegar

1 tablespoon honey

Sea salt, for garnish

MAKE AHEAD

You can prepare the glaze and stuff the figs several hours ahead of time, then pop them into the oven right before serving.

THIS IS A DELICIOUS SWEET-AND-SAVORY APPETIZER that pairs beautifully with a white or rosé wine in late summer or fall. The first time I made them I served them alongside a warm spinach salad on Thanksgiving, which was excellent. Otherwise, these are best served on small appetizer plates, as they become quite juicy. There's nothing too fussy here, just a simple combination of flavors that are perfect together.

1. Preheat the oven to 450°F.

2. In a small bowl, mix the ricotta, lemon juice, and thyme.

3. Snip the stem tips off the figs, then slice an X into the top of each fig so that they flower open in quarters, but do not cut through the last ¼ inch.

4. Spoon the ricotta mixture into each fig so that it fills it up and pops out of the top a bit.

5. In a small saucepan, heat the vinegar and the honey over medium heat until it forms a tangy and sweet glaze, 1 to 2 minutes.

6. Arrange the figs in a cupcake pan (which helps as they release their juices while cooking). Drizzle each fig with the balsamic-honey glaze, then sprinkle them with sea salt and place the pan in the oven. Roast until the tips of the figs become golden brown, 10 to 12 minutes. Serve the figs right away.

MINI CRAB CAKE LOLLIPOPS

MAKES ABOUT 24

1 large egg, beaten

½ cup finely chopped green onions

¼ cup finely crushed Ritz crackers
(can be reduced fat)

¼ cup minced red bell pepper

¼ cup chopped fresh parsley

3 tablespoons mayonnaise

1 tablespoon fresh lemon juice

1 teaspoon Dijon mustard,
plus more for serving

1 teaspoon Old Bay seasoning

¼ teaspoon Worcestershire sauce

16 ounces fresh crabmeat
(I buy fresh at Costco and use
claw meat, which has bigger chunks),
picked over for shells

Salt and freshly ground black pepper

Canola oil or nonstick cooking spray

Skewers or ice pop sticks

Mustard or Lemon-Dill Aioli Sauce
(recipe follows), for serving

THIS IS A TWIST ON THE EVER-POPULAR Ritz cracker crab cake. They're super easy and quick to make, but taste oh so gourmet. I love to serve them on skewers or small ice pop sticks, like lollipops, to make them easier to eat—and there's less to clean up.

1. In a large bowl, combine the egg, green onions, crackers, bell pepper, parsley, mayonnaise, lemon juice, mustard, Old Bay seasoning, and Worcestershire. Stir well to combine, then gently fold in the crabmeat, leaving large chunks. Season with salt and black pepper.

2. Shape into small crab cake patties, about 2 inches in diameter and arrange on a baking sheet. Cover and refrigerate for about 1 hour to allow the patties to firm up.

3. Heat a well-seasoned skillet over medium-high heat. Coat the skillet with canola oil, then fry the crab patties until golden brown, about 5 minutes on each side. (Alternatively, you can bake them to save calories and fat: Preheat the oven to 425°F. Spray a baking sheet with oil or nonstick spray. Bake until golden, about 10 minutes per side.)

4. Poke an ice pop stick or skewer into the middle of each crab cake, like a lollipop, and serve with a side of mustard or Lemon-Dill Aioli Sauce.

LEMON-DILL AIOLI SAUCE

MAKES 1½ CUPS

1 cup mayonnaise

¼ cup fresh lemon juice

2 tablespoons extra-virgin olive oil

1 tablespoon Dijon mustard

1 tablespoon chopped fresh dill

1 garlic clove, minced

Salt and freshly ground black pepper

This creamy sauce works beautifully with any fish dish.

In a small bowl, whisk together the mayonnaise, lemon juice, olive oil, mustard, dill, and garlic. Season with salt and pepper.

KALE CHIPS & ROASTED NUTTY CHICKPEAS

GLUTEN-FREE
VEGETARIAN
SERVES 4 TO 6

1 bunch kale, stemmed

Extra-virgin olive oil spray

2 pinches of kosher sea salt

1 (15.5-ounce) can chickpeas,
drained and rinsed

Pinch of garlic salt

Pinch of freshly ground black pepper

Pinch of sweet paprika

THESE CHIPS ARE TRULY THE ONLY WAY I can get my kids to come anywhere near kale. They love popping the crispy kale chips and chickpea "nuts" together in their mouths for a flavorful combination. For an extra-healthy protein-filled snack or lunch, you can add a poached egg on top, for what I call a "Bird's Nest."

1. Preheat the oven to 400°F.

2. Break the kale leaves into 2- to 4-inch pieces and thoroughly dry on paper towels.

3. Make the chips in batches. Arrange the leaves, not overlapping, on a large baking sheet and spray them lightly with olive oil spray. Season with the salt. Bake until crispy but not browned, about 8 minutes. You can flip the leaves if the bottoms haven't crisped enough. Remove and let cool on a large plate.

4. Lower the oven temperature to 350°F.

5. Dry the chickpeas with paper towels. Spread the chickpeas out on the baking sheet and spray them liberally with olive oil spray to coat. Season with the garlic salt, pepper, and paprika.

6. Bake until they are crispy and golden, 20 to 30 minutes. The moisture in canned chickpeas can vary widely, so check them frequently to prevent them from becoming overly dried out. If you like them to remain a little soft on the inside, cook them for less time.

7. Serve the crispy leaves and chickpeas together on a platter.

IN ADDITION TO THE RECIPES IN THIS CHAPTER, HERE ARE SOME EASY NO-BRAINERS THAT ARE POPULAR WITH MY CREW:

MANCHEGO/JAMÓN SERRANO TAPAS: Anybody can do a cheese platter with crackers and grapes. To step it up a bit, I layer toast points (or those small toast-shaped crackers my boys love) with squares of manchego cheese and pieces of jamón Serrano, then drizzle them with a balsamic reduction. I like to use six-month aged manchego because it's creamier and not as sharp or gamey tasting as manchego that's aged longer.

TO-ORDER GUACAMOLE: Now that I am living in the avocado state of California, I find there's nothing easier or better than tableside guacamole. I bought a few MOLCAJETES, which are like large mortar and pestles. I make the guacamole to order so it never becomes brown, and people can specify how much jalapeño or onion they like, for example. My kids don't care for really chunky guacamole so I tend to keep ours simple: 2 avocados, ½ small onion, chopped, a chopped tomato (these days it's the only way the kids will eat tomato), a lot of fresh cilantro, lemon and lime juice, as well as a little chili powder and salt—and a bit of cayenne if I want some heat.

FRESH SALSA: When my tomatoes are just getting a little overripe, I pop them into the food processor with some onions, cilantro, and jalapeño—or chipotle peppers for a smokier taste—to make fresh salsa. For a fruitier salsa I use whatever ripe, in-season fruit we have on hand, peach or pineapple or mango, for example. If I make it on a Sunday we eat it all week on everything from chips to eggs. My oldest son will go for chips and salsa or guacamole over most anything else as an after-school snack.

"PIG" WRAPS: Another classic, easy recipe is to wrap store-bought puff pastry over baked or grilled Polish sausages or mini hot dogs, then brush them with egg wash. (Or go ahead and use the croissant pastry that you can buy in a tube or can in the freezer section and wrap the triangles over the mini sausages!) Ten minutes in the oven at 325°F until golden brown and you've got that crowd-pleaser "pigs in a blanket" ready for some honey-mustard dipping.

MINI PIZZAS: To make no-fuss mini pizzas, I buy a few flatbreads and use a cookie cutter to create small circles for "crusts." We use jarred tomato sauce and then top it with oregano, mushrooms, and onions, then mozzarella—and I always add prosciutto on top of the ones meant for grown-ups. A few minutes under the broiler or in the toaster oven and they're ready.

ASIAN TURKEY MEATBALLS

MAKES ABOUT 24

SAUCE

3 tablespoons dark brown sugar

½ cup low-sodium soy sauce

½ cup sake

2 tablespoons minced fresh ginger

1 teaspoon toasted sesame oil

Pinch of red pepper flakes

1 green onion, thinly sliced

TURKEY MEATBALLS

Nonstick cooking spray

1 pound 93% lean ground turkey

¾ cup panko bread crumbs

¼ cup chopped fresh cilantro

1 large egg, beaten

2 green onions, chopped

2 garlic cloves, minced

1 tablespoon low-sodium soy sauce

1 teaspoon toasted sesame oil

Pinch of freshly ground black pepper

1 tablespoon sesame seeds, for serving

THE MEATBALL IS BACK, AND BETTER THAN EVER. Whether served as an appetizer or a meal, it's the perfect bite-size bit of comfort food. This recipe inspiration comes from one of the food trucks that we loved in Hoboken, New Jersey. They have about a dozen different varieties of meatballs daily, served up with delicious sides. I like to use ground turkey to keep the meatballs leaner; for even more flavor you could use beef or pork (or a combination). But the Asian glaze/dipping sauce makes this meatball a home run. I also keep the meatballs on the smaller side so they really soak up the sauce.

---

1. **Make the sauce:** In a small saucepan, combine ⅓ cup water and the brown sugar, stirring over medium heat until the sugar dissolves. Add the soy sauce, sake, ginger, sesame oil, and red pepper flakes. Reduce the heat to medium-low and gently simmer until the liquid has reduced by half, about 20 minutes. Set aside and stir in the green onion just before serving.

2. **Make the turkey meatballs:** Preheat the oven to 400°F. Coat a large baking sheet with nonstick spray.

3. In a large bowl, mix the turkey, bread crumbs, cilantro, egg, green onions, garlic, soy sauce, sesame oil, and black pepper. Using wet hands to prevent sticking, roll the mixture into mini meatballs about 1½ inches in diameter.

4. Place the meatballs on the prepared baking sheet and bake until thoroughly browned and cooked through, 7 to 8 minutes per side. Transfer to a platter.

5. When ready to serve, drizzle the meatballs with the sauce and sprinkle with the sesame seeds. Serve with toothpicks.

MAKE AHEAD

The morning of your event, make the sauce and form the meatballs, refrigerating them on a baking sheet to bake just before serving. These can also be cooked ahead and frozen on sheets; once frozen, bag them in freezer bags and heat and serve as needed.

SAUSAGE-STUFFED MUSHROOM CAPS

MAKES ABOUT 24

Vegetable oil, for the baking sheet

16 ounces button mushrooms

1 pound sweet Italian sausage, removed from casings, if necessary

¼ cup diced yellow onion

2 garlic cloves, minced

1 tablespoon fresh thyme leaves, or ¼ teaspoon dried

⅓ cup dry white wine or sherry

½ cup cream cheese or crème fraîche

1 large egg yolk

¼ cup panko bread crumbs

¼ cup freshly grated Parmesan cheese

1½ teaspoons dried parsley flakes

Pinch of red pepper flakes (optional)

THERE'S A FAMOUS TAPAS BAR in the old part of Madrid called El Mesón del Champiñón. It is all about the mushroom—which they make every which way, served with hunks of fresh French bread and amazing sangria. I have never met a mushroom I didn't like. This tapas-inspired appetizer becomes almost a meal in itself with about as much flavor as you can stuff inside a mushroom cap. You can prep these the day before, just pop them in the refrigerator on a covered tray. Then, 25 minutes before you're ready to serve, put them in the oven and enjoy straight away.

1. Preheat the oven to 425°F. Lightly oil a large baking sheet.

2. Clean the mushrooms and remove the stems. Dice the stems and reserve them for later.

3. In a large sauté pan, brown the sausage over medium-high heat, breaking it up as it cooks and stirring frequently, 6 to 8 minutes. Set aside on a plate; do not wipe out the pan.

4. In the same pan, heat the sausage grease over medium heat. Add the onion, garlic, and thyme and cook, stirring, until the onion is translucent, 3 to 5 minutes.

5. Add the diced mushroom stems and cook, stirring, until they soften, about 5 minutes. Add the wine and let it absorb and cook down a bit, about 4 minutes.

6. In a medium bowl, mix the cream cheese and egg yolk together, then stir in the panko, Parmesan, parsley flakes, and red pepper flakes (if using). Stir in the browned sausage and the mushroom-onion mixture.

7. Spoon the filling into the mushroom caps and arrange them on the prepared baking sheet. Bake the mushrooms until soft and cooked through, about 20 minutes, then turn the oven to broil and broil until golden on top, about 1 minute. Serve right away.

Family Dinners

POULTRY

What to make for dinner can be such a source of stress, and it's hard to please everyone. My picky kids are so difficult, sometimes it can take all the joy out of cooking. That's why I plan out my week of meals as much as possible, knowing how busy and frustrating it can all be if left to the last minute. I try to start each weekend by reviewing what I have for vegetables and meats. I then work out what I need to use and buy for a week of meals. I'm a leftovers lover, too, and I like to find many ways to repurpose what I've already made. Nothing fancy here, I promise. While some of my dinners may sound "exotic," they're pretty easy to make with ingredients that you can find at most grocery stores. If my kids could eat pizza or pasta every night, they would, but I do try to expand their palates and tastes for foods from many of the places I have lived in or traveled to. However, you'll find I keep it usually on the kid-friendly side (i.e., not using too many spicy ingredients or flavors I know for sure they won't go for). So don't get frustrated—get inspired!

SLOW-ROAST "FAUX-TISSERIE" CHICKEN

GLUTEN-FREE
SERVES 4

1 (4-pound) chicken
(free-range or very fresh)

1 tablespoon unsalted butter

½ teaspoon salt

½ teaspoon freshly ground black pepper

1 head garlic

1 lemon

1 bunch fresh thyme

1 bunch fresh rosemary

Butcher's twine, to truss the chicken

2 shallots, cut into thick wedges

1 cup halved baby red potatoes

1½ cups baby carrots

⅓ cup dry white wine

IF YOU WANT TO HAVE ONE SIGNATURE RECIPE, find a way to rock the roast chicken. Better than any takeout rotisserie, this one is cooked low and slow, "faux-tisserie" style. It's pretty hard to mess up, and in my opinion there is nothing more welcoming than the wafting smell of a delicious roast chicken to greet your family or guests. The secret is just patience and a little TLC, and you'll have a great meal. My kids love this chicken so much I make it almost every week.

Note that the roasted garlic bulb and lemon are mostly for added flavor and presentation, but the garlic is especially delicious when spread over a slice of crunchy crusty bread and drizzled with olive oil.

1. This technique is low and slow, so set your oven to 300°F early on and let it warm up as you start to prepare the chicken.

2. Thoroughly clean out the chicken and remove the giblets. (The giblets can be used for gravy, or I like to cook them and give them to my dog, Zara, as a treat. She loves roast chicken night!) Pat the chicken with paper towels until it is thoroughly dry. Liberally butter the top of the skin and under the skin, gently pulling the skin away off the breast and all around the chicken. Season with the salt and pepper on all sides.

3. Cut the garlic bulb in half crosswise and stuff half inside the cavity of the chicken, reserving the other half to roast in the pan. Cut the lemon in half and stuff half inside the cavity, reserving the other half to roast in the pan. Next take the thyme and rosemary and stuff the cavity with some of the herbs popping out, like a floral bouquet.

4. Now you are ready to truss or tie up the chicken, which allows it to cook evenly throughout. If you look online, there are so many ways to truss a chicken, leaving you wondering whether to tuck or not to tuck the wings or tie up the legs. Bottom line, the trick is to get the breast to pop. I like to lie the bird breast up and take the twine under the wings and over the top of the breast near the neck. Fold the skin in and tie the string once. Then run the string along the front of the breast, tucking the wings under it and over the bottom of the breast. Cross tie once in front and then wrap the strings around the back and over the thighs. Here you can pull the string taut over the thighs and then tie the legs together (optional) by crisscrossing the strings around the drumsticks with the herbal bouquet sticking out slightly underneath. Put the chicken in a roasting pan.

5. Toss the other half of the garlic head as well as the remaining half lemon into the pan. Add the shallot wedges. Cover the pan with aluminum foil and roast the chicken for about 2 hours. Remove the foil and add the baby potatoes and carrots to the pan. Scoop any juices with a ladle or spoon and pour over the chicken and vegetables, then pour over the wine. Roast, uncovered, for 1 hour more, until the chicken is golden brown and registers 180°F on an instant-read thermometer.

6. Remove the chicken from the pan and let rest for 10 minutes. Carve the chicken and serve along with the roast potatoes, carrots, and shallot, ladling over some of the fragrant jus from the bottom of the pan.

Note: The rule of thumb is usually 20 minutes per pound, but that's at 325°F. So when slow roasting at 300°F, I let it go longer, around 2½ to 3 hours for a 4-pound bird, give or take.

NEXT-DAY MEALS

Again, the best part is the leftovers. Besides the perfect chicken dinner, I make a great chicken Cobb salad (page 54), chicken enchiladas verdes (page 203), chicken noodle soup, mushroom and chicken risotto, chicken and veggie stir-fry, chicken and pasta fettuccine—you get the idea . . . Chicken a thousand ways—which picky eaters like mine usually love! And don't throw away the carcass of the chicken once you've eaten all the meat. It can be simmered in water to make homemade chicken broth. Nothing goes to waste with this recipe.

CHICKEN TAGINE

GLUTEN-FREE
SERVES 6

1 tablespoon ground coriander

1 tablespoon ground turmeric

1 teaspoon ground cinnamon

1 teaspoon ground cumin

1 teaspoon ground ginger

1 teaspoon sweet paprika

5 tablespoons extra-virgin olive oil

2 garlic cloves, chopped

3 pounds bone-in skinless chicken thighs (about 6)

1 medium yellow onion, chopped

1 head cauliflower, cut into florets

2 cups chicken broth

1 tablespoon tomato paste

1 tablespoon grated fresh ginger

1 bay leaf

1 (15-ounce) can chickpeas, drained and rinsed

1 cup prunes or dried apricots

½ cup green olives (optional)

Salt and freshly ground black pepper

Chopped fresh cilantro leaves, for garnish

Cooked basmati rice, quinoa, or couscous, for serving

I LOVE TO READ ABOUT FOOD, and I scan everything I can get my hands on for new things to try. In fact, the idea for making this dish came from spotting a beautifully prepared tagine in a Williams-Sonoma catalog. It seemed very doable and like something my family would enjoy, so I set out to make it my way, pulling back a bit on the spice so my kids would still eat it. While this dish is Moroccan in origin, the combination of savory and sweet is a Spanish and Latin hallmark as well. Latinas love to combine raisins and almonds, for example, bringing tanginess and sweetness together.

1. Preheat the oven to 350°F.

2. In a small bowl, combine the coriander, turmeric, cinnamon, cumin, ginger, and paprika. Stir in 2 tablespoons of the olive oil and the garlic to create a paste. Coat the chicken with the paste and set aside.

3. In a large skillet, heat 1 tablespoon of the olive oil over medium heat. Add the onion and cook, stirring frequently, until soft, about 5 minutes. Remove the onion and set aside. In the same skillet, heat another tablespoon of the olive oil and add the cauliflower. Cook, stirring occasionally, until the cauliflower begins to brown, 8 to 10 minutes. Return the onion to the skillet and set aside.

4. In a Dutch oven or tagine pot, heat the remaining 1 tablespoon olive oil over medium-high heat. Add the chicken thighs and cook until browned on both sides, about 8 minutes total. Deglaze the pot with the broth, stirring to scrape up any browned bits on the bottom of the pot, then add the tomato paste, ginger, and bay leaf. Cook until the liquid has reduced by about a quarter, about 8 minutes, then add the onion and cauliflower mixture and

the chickpeas. Reduce the heat to medium-low and simmer, covered, for 15 minutes. Add the prunes (or use both prunes and apricots for a sweeter tagine) and olives. Season with salt and

pepper. Transfer the Dutch oven to the oven and cook, covered, for 10 minutes more.

5. Serve garnished with cilantro on a bed of basmati rice.

POLLO AL AJILLO (Chicken in Garlic Sauce)

GLUTEN-FREE
SERVES 4

1 (4-pound) whole chicken

¼ cup extra-virgin olive oil

10 garlic cloves, unpeeled

2 sprigs fresh rosemary

2 sprigs fresh thyme

½ teaspoon smoked paprika

Pinch of kosher salt

Pinch of freshly ground black pepper

1 cup dry white wine or dry sherry

2 tablespoons chopped fresh parsley, for garnish

HERE'S A SPANISH CLASSIC that I loved so much growing up in Madrid. It's practically a national delicacy, served in most restaurants or bars throughout all of Spain. And *pollo al ajillo* (pronounced *POY-yo al a-HEE-yo*) is such an easy, flavorful, and quick dish to make. It's also a one-pot wonder, with so little cleanup. Have some fresh country bread on hand to sop up the garlic sauce! Yum. That's what my kids love the most about this recipe. Serve it with Spanish-style potatoes (very thinly sliced new potatoes fried in olive oil) and a delicious green salad or side of green vegetables.

1. Chop the chicken into 8 serving pieces or fist-size chunks. Leave the bones in, but remove the skin from all but the wings. (However, if you don't mind the extra fat, the skin does add more flavor.)

2. In a large Dutch oven, heat the olive oil over medium heat. Toss in the garlic cloves and allow them caramelize, stirring continuously, for about 5 minutes, being careful not to let them burn. With a slotted spoon, remove the garlic from the oil and set aside.

3. To the garlic-flavored oil, add the chicken and the sprigs of rosemary and thyme. Cook the chicken until it is golden on all sides and cooked through, about 15 minutes total, keeping a watchful eye over the chicken and turning it frequently to prevent burning.

4. Using a paper towel, soak up some of the excess oil in the pot, then return the garlic to the pot. Season the chicken with the smoked paprika, salt, and pepper.

5. Pour in the wine and let it reduce until it has almost completely cooked off, about 10 minutes.

6. Remove the chicken and plate it, pouring any pan juices over the top, then garnish with the chopped parsley and serve.

Note: If you are uncomfortable chopping up the whole chicken on your own, have your butcher chop it into 8 pieces for you.

ARROZ CON POLLO Y GANDULES
(Chicken & Rice with Spanish Peas)

GLUTEN-FREE
SERVES 4 TO 6

1 (4- to 5-pound) whole chicken, cut into 8 pieces, skin on

Salt and freshly ground black pepper

2 tablespoons extra-virgin olive oil

1 medium Vidalia or Spanish onion, minced

2 garlic cloves, minced

1 (14.5-ounce) can diced tomatoes with juices

1 tablespoon tomato paste

1 packet Goya Sazón Culantro y Achiote (can be found in Spanish food section or on Amazon)

1 teaspoon Tabasco or other hot sauce (optional)

1 bay leaf

½ teaspoon ground cumin

Pinch of saffron

3 cups chicken broth

1 cup dry white wine

2 cups short-grain white rice (I like Spanish Bomba rice)

1 (15-ounce) can gandules (flat Spanish green peas), drained and rinsed, or 1 cup frozen green peas

Chopped fresh parsley, for garnish

THIS CHICKEN-AND-RICE ONE-POT DINNER IS A STROLL DOWN MEMORY LANE. Every time I make it, I am reminded of my *abuelita* in Puerto Rico; it was a family favorite then and it is still now.

1. Preheat the oven to 400°F.

2. Season the chicken with salt and pepper.

3. In a deep oven-safe or cast-iron skillet, heat the olive oil over medium-high heat. Add the chicken and cook, stirring frequently, until browned on both sides, about 10 minutes total. (It doesn't have to be completely cooked as the chicken will cook more in the rice later.) Remove the chicken from the pan and set aside.

4. Add the onion and garlic to the skillet and cook, stirring, until softened, about 5 minutes.

5. Add the tomatoes with their juices, tomato paste, packet of Culantro y Achiote, Tabasco (if using), bay leaf, cumin, and saffron and simmer, stirring frequently, for 5 minutes more.

6. Add the broth and wine and bring the liquids to a boil. Stir in the rice and cook for 5 minutes. Add the chicken, along with the gandules.

7. Transfer to the oven and bake, uncovered, for about 30 minutes, until the rice is cooked and the liquids have been absorbed.

8. Serve on a large plate, garnished with parsley.

Note: There are so many ways to make this dish, and I've made mine more kid friendly, without too much spiciness. One or two seeded and minced serrano chiles and ½ cup or so of sliced Spanish olives can be added to give it more Spanish flavor.

COQ AU VIN

SERVES 4 TO 6

¼ cup all-purpose flour

1 (4- to 5-pound) chicken, cut into 8 pieces

Kosher salt and freshly ground black pepper

1 tablespoon extra-virgin olive oil

½ cup chopped pancetta (or slab bacon cut into small cubes)

1 tablespoon unsalted butter

1½ cups sliced cremini mushrooms

1 yellow onion, cut into 2-inch chunks

3 cups dry full-bodied red wine, like a Burgundy or Bordeaux

1 cup chicken broth

1 tablespoon tomato paste

3 large carrots, cut into ½-inch pieces

2 celery stalks, cut into 1-inch pieces

6 sprigs fresh thyme

5 sprigs rosemary

2 garlic cloves, minced

2 bay leaves

1 cup frozen small pearl onions

I JOKE THAT I MAKE CHICKEN A THOUSAND WAYS, because it's what my family eats the most, with no complaints. This, though, may be our favorite—a classic coq au vin, or chicken in wine sauce. It's hearty and delicious, perfect for a cool fall or winter night with a glass of red wine. My philosophy while making this dish: A little wine for the chicken, and a little for me. Serve it up with some roasted or mashed potatoes or some wild rice to soak up the delicious juices.

---

1. Preheat the oven to 300°F.

2. Put the flour on a plate. Dry the chicken and season it with salt and pepper. Dredge the chicken pieces in the flour, fully covering all the pieces.

3. In a large Dutch oven or heavy oven-safe pot with a lid, heat the olive oil over medium heat. Add the pancetta and cook, stirring frequently, until it is browned, about 6 minutes. Using a slotted spoon, remove the pancetta and set aside.

4. Add the chicken to the pot, in batches, if necessary. Cook until browned evenly on all sides, about 8 minutes total. Remove the chicken and set aside.

5. Melt the butter in the pot. Add the mushrooms and onion and cook, stirring continuously, until the mushrooms release their juices and the onion begins to soften, about 7 minutes. Remove all from the pan.

6. To deglaze the pot, pour in 1 cup of the wine and the broth and then stir in the tomato paste.

7. Return the chicken to the pot along with the pancetta, mushroom and onion mixture, carrots, celery, thyme and rosemary sprigs, garlic, bay leaves, and the remaining 2 cups wine. Cover the pot, transfer to the oven, and bake until the chicken is just cooked through, about 30 minutes.

8. Put the pot back on the stovetop, uncover, and bring the stew to a simmer. Add the pearl onions and cook until tender, another 10 minutes. Remove the bay leaf and herb sprigs. Season with salt and pepper. Bon appétit!

CHICKEN KORMA KEBABS

GLUTEN-FREE
SERVES 4 TO 6

2 cups plain 2% Greek yogurt

1 cup reduced-fat coconut milk

2 tablespoons honey

2 tablespoons fresh lime juice

2 tablespoons korma curry paste
(such as Patak's, available on Amazon)

1 garlic clove, minced

1 teaspoon minced fresh ginger

½ teaspoon salt

Pinch of freshly ground black pepper

2 pounds chicken breast,
cut lengthwise into thin strips

Nonstick cooking spray

3 tablespoons crushed peanuts or almonds

3 tablespoons chopped fresh cilantro

Lime wedges, for serving

Indian flatbread, for serving (optional)

THESE ARE NOT YOUR AVERAGE CHICKEN KEBABS, which can be so ordinary. I like cooking with curry and coconut milk, and this is a delicious combination of both. A yogurt marinade keeps the kebabs nice and moist, and cools down the curry kick just a bit. These are delicious cooked over the grill and a really nice appetizer or meal.

1. In a large glass or nonreactive bowl, stir together the yogurt, coconut milk, honey, lime juice, curry paste, garlic, ginger, salt, and pepper. Put the chicken slices in the mixture, turning to coat them on all sides, cover, and marinate in the refrigerator for at least 4 hours, or, even better, overnight.

2. Thread the chicken onto metal or wooden kebab sticks (if wooden, soak them for at least 30 minutes to prevent burning).

3. Heat a grill or griddle to medium-high and spray with nonstick spray. Grill the chicken strips until cooked through, 2 to 3 minutes on each side.

4. Plate the kebabs and sprinkle the crushed nuts on top. Garnish with the chopped cilantro and serve with lime wedges and Indian flatbread, if desired.

Note: This dish requires a minimum of 4 hours marinating time.

CHICKEN-PINE NUT LETTUCE WRAPS

SERVES 4

STIR-FRY SAUCE

2 tablespoons plus 1 teaspoon
low-sodium soy sauce

1 tablespoon rice vinegar

1 teaspoon dark brown sugar

1 teaspoon toasted sesame oil

¼ cup chopped green onions

3 garlic cloves, minced

½ teaspoon minced fresh ginger

CHICKEN AND PINE NUTS

2 tablespoons extra-virgin olive oil

2 large chicken breasts (about 1 pound),
cut into small pieces

½ cup minced red onion

1 celery stalk, diced

¼ cup chopped canned water chestnuts

¼ cup pine nuts

Salt and freshly ground black pepper

¼ cup chopped fresh cilantro

1 head iceberg lettuce or butter lettuce,
for serving

MY LETTUCE WRAPS ARE INSPIRED by the ones you find at P.F. Chang's, which my family loves but which are really not all that healthy. I created my own slightly healthier version, which are great as appetizers or as a light lunch or dinner.

---

1. **Make the sauce:** In a small bowl, whisk together the soy sauce, vinegar, sugar, sesame oil, green onions, garlic, and ginger. Set aside.

2. **Make the chicken and pine nuts:** In a large skillet, heat the olive oil over medium-high heat. Add the chicken pieces and cook, stirring occasionally, until partially cooked, about 4 minutes. Remove and set aside.

3. Add the onion, celery, water chestnuts, and stir-fry sauce to the skillet and cook, stirring, until the onion starts to soften, about 3 minutes.

4. Using a slotted spoon, add the chicken and pine nuts, minus any liquid that the chicken has released, to the skillet and cook, stirring, until the chicken is cooked through, 2 to 3 minutes more. Season with salt and pepper.

5. When ready to serve, stir in the cilantro. Carefully separate the lettuce leaves and arrange them on plates or a platter. Spoon the mixture into each of the lettuce cups/wraps and serve.

GREEK CHICKEN KEBABS

GLUTEN-FREE
SERVES 2 TO 4

1 cup plain 2% Greek yogurt

½ teaspoon grated lemon zest

1 tablespoon fresh lemon juice

1 tablespoon tomato paste

1 garlic clove, minced

1 tablespoon chopped fresh parsley

1 tablespoon minced fresh oregano,
or ½ teaspoon dried

½ teaspoon fresh thyme leaves,
or ⅛ teaspoon dried

½ teaspoon chopped fresh rosemary,
or ¼ teaspoon dried

Salt and freshly ground black pepper

1 pound chicken breasts, cut into
1-inch cubes

Nonstick cooking spray

Greek Tzatziki Sauce (recipe follows)

Note: Plan ahead, as this recipe
requires 2 hours to marinate.

WORKING MY WAY THROUGH MY LOADS OF CHICKEN RECIPES, this is another family favorite. These Greek chicken kebabs are no-fail, and perfect for middle-of-the-week craziness (well, all times really) when you need something easy that everyone will love. The key is letting the chicken marinate for a couple of hours in the yogurt sauce to keep it moist and seal in the flavors. Also, using fresh herbs to flavor up the yogurt is preferable, but dry herbs work just fine, too.

My favorite way to serve this is with Horiatiki (page 224) or any fresh salad, pita, hummus (page 36), and homemade tzatziki sauce (recipe follows).

1. In a large bowl, stir together the yogurt, lemon zest, lemon juice, tomato paste, garlic, parsley, oregano, thyme, rosemary, and a pinch each of salt and pepper.

2. Stir the chicken into the yogurt mixture. Cover and marinate in the refrigerator overnight, if you can, or for at least 2 hours.

3. Heat a grill or griddle to medium and spray with nonstick spray.

4. Skewer the chicken pieces one by one onto four metal skewers or wooden kebab sticks (if wooden, soak them for at least 30 minutes to prevent burning).

5. Grill or griddle the chicken until golden, after about 5 minutes, then turn the skewers. The chicken is done when the juices run clear, 10 to 15 minutes total.

GREEK TZATZIKI SAUCE

GLUTEN-FREE
MAKES ABOUT 2½ CUPS

1 cup plain Greek yogurt

1 medium cucumber, peeled, halved, and seeded

Salt

2 garlic cloves, crushed

2 tablespoons fresh lemon juice

1 tablespoon extra-virgin olive oil

1 teaspoon minced fresh oregano

1 teaspoon finely chopped fresh mint leaves (or dill, if you prefer)

THIS IS THE PERFECT PARTNER to the Greek chicken on page 103 or any grilled meat or fish made in a similar style. It's also a delicious dipping sauce for veggies served cold or grilled, and always with a side of pita. You can easily buy tzatziki, but I prefer homemade, as it is so easy to make and always better served fresh. For a very garlicky tzatziki, use 1 or 2 more garlic cloves.

1. If you would like a very thick, creamier consistency, drain the yogurt in cheesecloth in a strainer set over a bowl until most of the liquid has drained off, about 1 hour.

2. Grate the cucumber, then put it in a sieve or in cheesecloth. Squeeze and press out any excess water. Salt the cucumber.

3. In a medium bowl, whisk together the yogurt, garlic, lemon juice, and olive oil. Stir in the cucumber, oregano, and mint. Season with salt. Refrigerate until ready to serve.

GRILLED VEGGIE SKEWERS

If you would like to serve the kebabs with skewered vegetables, I recommend grilling them separately. The vegetables always cook faster than the chicken, thus, if you skewer them both together, one or the other will be overcooked. I like to thread skewers with a combination of whole trimmed mushrooms, red or green bell pepper and/or zucchini cut into large chunks, and red onion cut to a similar size. Just brush with olive oil and flavor with salt, pepper, and mix of fresh or dried herbs, such as oregano and thyme, and grill, rotating the skewers occasionally, for about 8 minutes.

TURKEY BOLOGNESE & SPAGHETTI SQUASH

GLUTEN-FREE
SERVES 6

1 large spaghetti squash

4 tablespoons extra-virgin olive oil

Salt and freshly ground black pepper

1 medium yellow onion, diced

2 celery stalks, diced

2 carrots, diced

1 pound ground turkey (93% lean is fine—any less fat and it becomes too dry and flavorless)

2 garlic cloves, crushed

1 tablespoon fresh oregano, or 1 teaspoon dried

Pinch of red pepper flakes

1 (8-ounce) package cremini mushrooms, diced

½ cup red wine

2 tablespoons tomato paste

1 (28-ounce) can whole peeled tomatoes, drained

1 cup chicken broth

2 tablespoons heavy cream

¼ cup chopped fresh basil, for garnish

½ cup freshly grated Parmesan cheese

IF YOU LOVE PASTA AS MUCH AS I DO, there is nothing quite like a hearty plate of spaghetti with a chunky meat Bolognese sauce. While my family will have the real deal occasionally, and I don't believe in depriving them of one of their favorite foods, I do think this is a great alternative. It has become a popular middle-of-the-week meal in our home because it is so simple to make, and I love that it is loaded with vegetables and healthy ingredients; it's a sneaky way to get my kids to eat their veggies.

Spaghetti squash is a good substitute for pasta, and it's loaded with fiber and so low calorie! The squash "noodles" soak up the sauce and add their own texture and flavor, so you'll hardly miss the pasta. As for the Bolognese, you won't miss the beef much once you season up the ground turkey and add in all the flavorings and spices to enhance it—it tastes like the real deal.

1. Preheat the oven to 375°F.

2. Cook the whole spaghetti squash in the microwave for 5 minutes to allow it to soften a bit, which will make cutting through it easier.

3. When the squash has cooled enough to handle, cut it in half lengthwise. Clean out the seeds with a fork, then drizzle each half with 1 tablespoon of the olive oil. Season with salt and pepper, then place the halves cut-side up on a baking sheet and bake until you see the squash soften up, about 45 minutes.

recipe continues

4. While the squash is cooking, in a large skillet, heat the remaining 2 tablespoons olive oil over medium-high heat. Add the onion, celery, and carrot and a pinch of salt. Cook, stirring frequently, until the vegetables are softened, about 5 minutes.

5. Stir in the ground turkey and garlic. Using a wooden spoon, break up the turkey and cook until no longer pink, about 5 minutes. Season with oregano, red pepper flakes, and salt and black pepper to taste. Stir in the mushrooms and cook, stirring occasionally, until starting to soften, about 2 minutes.

6. Pour the wine into a measuring cup, then mix in the tomato paste. Pour the wine mixture over the turkey mixture and simmer to reduce slightly, about 4 minutes. Add the tomatoes, using your wooden spoon to break them apart.

7. Add the broth and cream and stir into the meat sauce to blend. Simmer to allow the sauce to thicken and the flavors to meld, 8 to 10 minutes.

8. Stir in the basil and ¼ cup of the Parmesan, then season with additional salt and black pepper.

9. Remove the squash from the oven and let it sit until cool enough to handle. Using a fork, scrape out the strands of "noodles" and put them in a large serving bowl.

10. Spoon the Bolognese over the spaghetti squash "noodles" and sprinkle with the remaining ¼ cup Parmesan.

MOROCCAN TURKEY CHILI

GLUTEN-FREE
SERVES 8 TO 10

2 tablespoons extra-virgin olive oil

1 medium yellow onion, diced

2 garlic cloves, minced

2 pounds 93% lean ground turkey

Kosher salt and freshly ground black pepper

2 tablespoons ras el hanout (see Sidebar)

2 tablespoons chili powder

1 teaspoon ground cinnamon

1 teaspoon ground cumin

1 teaspoon dried oregano

1 (28-ounce) can diced tomatoes with juices

2 cups chicken broth

2 tablespoons tomato paste

2 sweet potatoes, peeled and cut into ¼-inch pieces

½ red bell pepper, cut into ½-inch chunks

½ yellow bell pepper, cut into ½-inch chunks

2 celery stalks, cut into ½-inch pieces

1 zucchini, cut into 1-inch cubes

1 (12-ounce) can cannellini beans, drained and rinsed

1 (12-ounce) can chickpeas, drained and rinsed

Pinch of red pepper flakes (optional)

½ cup chopped fresh cilantro, for garnish

WEEKENDS ARE WHEN I REALLY GET TO SPEND TIME IN THE KITCHEN. I like to make hearty soups, stews, and sauces that I know the family will enjoy all week long. Having a well-stocked fridge with meals ready to eat makes my life during the week so much easier, and will make yours easier, too! But you don't want to spend your entire weekend over a hot stove, so one of my favorite kitchen tools is my slow cooker. I just toss everything into the pot and then go . . . leaving it to do all the work.

This is one of those great weekend inventions, which has a Middle Eastern zest with the addition of ras el hanout and chickpeas. It's comfort food with a nutritious kick of protein and vegetables—and no guilt. I like to serve this with pita bread on the side, over rice, or just on its own, topped with shredded cheese, sour cream, and some sliced avocado. It also makes for great leftovers and lunch on the go.

1. In a slow cooker or large skillet (if you're using a slow cooker set first to sauté function, and if you don't have a sauté option, then use a skillet), warm the olive oil over medium-high heat. Add the onion and garlic and cook, stirring, until the onion is translucent, 5 to 7 minutes. Add the ground turkey and cook, stirring, until lightly browned, 6 to 8 minutes. Season with salt and black pepper. Turn the slow cooker to Low (transfer everything to the slow cooker now, if you've been using a skillet), add the ras el hanout, chili powder, cinnamon, cumin, and oregano and stir into the meat, letting it all absorb. Add the diced tomatoes with juices, broth, 1 cup water, and the tomato paste and cook for 2½ hours.

recipe continues

Note: The total time to make this recipe is 4½ hours, using a slow cooker on Low.

2. Stir in the sweet potatoes, bell peppers, celery, and zucchini (these vegetables are best when they are a still a bit crunchy, that's why I add them later). Add the beans and chickpeas, cover, and cook on Low until the sweet potato is tender, about 2 hours more. If you like more heat to your chili, you can add a pinch of red pepper flakes.

3. Top with the cilantro when serving.

NO SLOW COOKER? NO SWEAT.

If you don't have a slow cooker, do not despair. This recipe can easily be made in a Dutch oven or large soup pot, simmering over medium-high heat in half the time. Just add the sweet potatoes midway through and save the crunchy veggies and beans for the last 10 minutes.

Ras El Hanout is a North African/Moroccan spice mix. You can find it in Middle Eastern stores or online, and it's becoming fairly common in mainstream American grocery stores as well. It's a mix of more than a dozen aromatic spices, so if you are a purist and want to make your own, try blending ground cardamom, ground cloves, ground cumin, ground cinnamon, grated nutmeg, ground ginger, ground chile, ground coriander, black pepper, ground turmeric, ground mace, fenugreek, paprika and—if you like a hint of licorice—a tiny pinch of ground fennel seeds. (You can also grind the whole spices and then combine them to make the spice mix.) Toast the mixed blend in a small skillet over low heat to boost the flavor and aroma. Ras el hanout is fantastic on all meats as a seasoning or rub, and adds a really warm and inviting flavor. I especially love to use it in chili, stews, and soups or Middle Eastern tagines. I've read that in Morocco they actually believe it is an aphrodisiac spice, so use it liberally.

PAELLA WITH CHICKEN & SAUSAGE

GLUTEN-FREE
SERVES 8 TO 10

1 (3½ pound) chicken, cut into 3-inch pieces using a cleaver, or 2 pounds chicken thighs, cut into 3-inch chunks

6 tablespoons extra-virgin olive oil

Salt and freshly ground black pepper

1 tablespoon chopped fresh oregano

1 tablespoon smoked paprika

1 teaspoon ground turmeric

2 cups uncooked Bomba or other short-grain white rice

3 garlic cloves, minced

1 quart (32 ounces) chicken broth

Grated zest of 1 lemon

2 tablespoons fresh lemon juice

1 tablespoon tomato paste

½ teaspoon saffron threads

2 bay leaves

1 cup chopped white or Spanish onion

1 red bell pepper, coarsely chopped

½ pound fresh chorizo sausage, removed from casings and crumbled or cut up

2 cups fresh or frozen green peas

½ bunch fresh parsley, chopped

½ teaspoon red pepper flakes

INSPIRED STRAIGHT FROM MY YEARS OF LIVING IN SPAIN, I keep this one family-friendly, as my kids and husband aren't into fish. I wish they were, because I love a traditional *paella Valenciana*, with its aromatic combination of mussels, clams, fish, and chorizo. However, this will be equally yummy and easier, in fact, to make. You can always add any fish and shrimp of your choice.

The other benefit to making this paella is that it's great for entertaining, serving a lot of people and looking so spectacular as the central dish. In fact, Joe's fortieth birthday party had a Spanish theme and this was the main entrée, which everyone loved. I also like that it's pretty easy to make and low maintenance, meaning not a lot of steps. So you can pretty much cook it in front of the crowd, serve appetizers and drinks for an hour as it cooks, then serve it up straight from the paella pan.

1. Put the chicken pieces in a large bowl. Drizzle 2 tablespoons of the olive oil on top of the chicken, then season with salt and black pepper. Mix in the oregano, paprika, and turmeric. Toss to coat all the chicken pieces, then refrigerate as you prepare the rice.

2. In a paella pan or extra-large skillet, heat 2 tablespoons of the olive oil over medium heat, then stir in the rice and garlic. Coat the rice grains with the olive oil and garlic until fragrant and shiny, about 2 minutes. Then stir in the broth, lemon zest, lemon juice, tomato paste, saffron, and bay leaves, mixing well.

3. Bring the mixture to a boil, then reduce the heat to medium-low. Cook, covered, for about 25 minutes.

Note: While I have included an option here to use boneless thighs, the bones really add to the flavor of this dish. You can ask your butcher to cut the chicken into 3-inch pieces, or try it yourself with a heavy knife—it's not as hard as it sounds.

4. As the rice is cooking, in another skillet or Dutch oven, heat 2 tablespoons of the olive oil over medium heat. Add the onion, bell pepper, and chicken to the pan. Brown the chicken pieces on all sides, for a total of about 10 minutes (5 minutes if using boneless thighs). Add the sausage pieces and brown with the chicken until the meat is cooked through, 8 to 10 minutes more.

5. Stir the chicken and sausage mixture and the peas into the rice for the last 5 minutes of cooking. Garnish with the parsley and red pepper flakes. Serve immediately, straight from the pan.

TURKEY CABBAGE ROLLS

GLUTEN-FREE
SERVES 8

Vegetable oil, for the baking dish

1 head green cabbage

2 tablespoons extra-virgin olive oil

½ cup diced white onion

Salt

2 garlic cloves, minced

1 (28-ounce) can crushed tomatoes

2 tablespoons tomato paste

1 tablespoon balsamic vinegar

1 tablespoon chopped fresh oregano,
or 1 teaspoon dried

2 teaspoons sugar (optional)

Freshly ground black pepper

1½ pounds ground turkey (93% lean)

1 cup cooked brown rice (prepared
according to the package instructions)

1 cup cooked quinoa (prepared according
to the package instructions)

½ cup grated carrots

½ cup minced white mushrooms

½ cup 2% milk

½ cup freshly grated Parmesan cheese,
plus more for serving

1 large egg

1 tablespoon Worcestershire sauce

MY MOM MAKES DELICIOUS CABBAGE ROLLS, but when I ask her for the recipe, she can never tell me exactly what goes into it. That's how my mom cooks! But I have watched her make them, and while she usually uses ground beef and white rice, I wanted to try a healthier version using ground turkey, quinoa, and brown rice, while adding some grated vegetables like carrots and mushrooms to flavor and bind the turkey even more. This is a low-fat, low-calorie, diet-friendly meal. When I have leftovers (which I usually have to hide so my husband doesn't get to them first), I love to pack it up for my lunch during the week and just reheat it in a microwave. It almost always tastes better after a day or two when the sauce has soaked into the filling.

1. Preheat the oven to 350°F. Lightly oil a large baking dish.

2. Bring a large pot of water to boil, then, using tongs or two forks, carefully slide in the whole head of the cabbage. Cook long enough to soften up the leaves, about 10 minutes. Remove the cabbage and set it aside to cool.

3. In a large saucepot, heat the olive oil over medium heat. Add ¼ cup of the onion and a pinch of salt and cook, stirring, until soft, about 2 minutes. Add the garlic and cook, stirring, for 30 seconds. Add the crushed tomatoes, tomato paste, vinegar, oregano, and sugar (if using). Let the sauce simmer and thicken for about 30 minutes. Season with salt and pepper.

4. In a large bowl, mix the ground turkey, rice, quinoa, the carrots, mushrooms, milk, Parmesan, remaining ¼ cup onion, egg, and Worcestershire and season with salt and pepper. Set aside.

5. One by one, remove the cabbage leaves and cut the hard stem out from the middle, making a V-shaped cut. This will allow you to roll the leaves more easily over the filling.

6. To make the cabbage rolls, put about 2 tablespoons (plus) of the filling in the center of each leaf. Fold each side over the V-shaped incision and roll up the leaves. Arrange the rolls side-by-side, seam-side down in the prepared baking dish—you should have around 14 rolls.

7. Sprinkle 2 tablespoons water into the dish and cover tightly with aluminum foil. Bake for 30 minutes, then remove from the oven. Remove the foil and carefully drain the accumulated liquid from the dish. Top the rolls with the sauce and cook, uncovered, for 30 minutes more. Sprinkle with Parmesan cheese and serve.

HEALTHY & HEARTY "CLEAN OUT THE FRIDGE" PASTA

SERVES 6

1 pound whole wheat pasta (spaghetti, orecchiette or penne)

1 lemon

4 or 5 links precooked sweet Italian chicken sausage (12 ounces)

1 tablespoon extra-virgin olive oil

1 bunch kale, tough stems and ribs removed, or Broccolini, trimmed and coarsely chopped

1 shallot, finely chopped

8 ounces white button mushrooms, sliced

1 (15.5-ounce) can cannellini beans, drained and rinsed

1 cup cherry tomatoes, halved

½ cup dry white wine

Grated zest of 1 lemon

Juice of 1 lemon

½ teaspoon dried oregano

½ cup diced ricotta salata cheese (¼-inch cubes; optional)

½ cup freshly grated Parmesan cheese

ONE NIGHT, WHEN JOE WAS ABOUT TO RUSH OUT THE DOOR to a soccer game, I concocted this pasta out of what we had in the refrigerator. There were lots of veggies that needed to be used up, and I wanted to make a more nutritious and hearty dish, hence the whole wheat pasta, chicken sausage, and kale. I added canned beans, cherry tomatoes, and mushrooms to push it further into a hearty vegetable stew category, and ricotta salata for flavor (you can leave it out, if you like). Now this recipe is one of my husband's favorite weeknight meals—it's quick, easy, and healthy! Sauté the veggies and chicken sausage while the pasta cooks, and dinner is on the table in 20 minutes.

1. Bring a large pot of water to a boil. Cook the pasta according to the package directions, reserve ½ cup of the pasta cooking water, and drain.

3. In a medium skillet, cook the sausages over medium-high heat, turning occasionally, until browned and cooked through, 8 to 10 minutes. Let cool slightly, then thinly slice the sausages. Set aside.

4. In large saucepot, heat the olive oil over medium heat. Add the kale and shallot and cook, stirring, until kale softens a bit, 2 to 4 minutes. Add the sausage, mushrooms, beans, cherry tomatoes, wine, and lemon juice. Simmer, stirring occasionally, until the mushrooms and tomatoes are tender, 4 to 6 minutes. Sprinkle in the oregano.

5. Add the drained pasta to the pot with kale mixture. Stir in ricotta salata (if using), the Parmesan, and the reserved pasta cooking water, tossing until well mixed. To serve, sprinkle with the lemon zest.

Variation I have also made this using "zoodles," or spiralized zucchini noodles, which makes this recipe even healthier by cutting down the carbs!

BEEF

SLOW-COOKER ROPA VIEJA

GLUTEN-FREE
SERVES 6 TO 8

1½ pounds flank steak

Sazón seasoning, such as Goya Sazón

1 medium yellow onion, thinly sliced

½ cup thinly sliced red bell pepper

½ cup thinly sliced green bell pepper

1 (14-ounce) can crushed tomatoes

1 cup beef broth

2 tablespoons tomato paste

1 tablespoon red wine vinegar

2 garlic cloves, minced

1 tablespoon dried oregano

1 tablespoon ground cumin

½ bottle beer, such as a pale ale

Tabasco sauce (optional)

1 cup halved pimiento-stuffed Manzanilla olives (optional)

Chopped fresh cilantro, for garnish

Notes: Sazón is a Spanish seasoning found in Latin aisle (Goya makes a popular version)—or if you can't find it, a combination of salt, pepper, and garlic salt will do. • If you prefer a crispier ropa vieja, you can sear the flank steak first in 2 tablespoons olive oil before placing it in the slow cooker.

BEEF IS ANOTHER FAMILY FAVORITE that I can serve with no complaints, and no matter how it's prepared it's generally an easy dinner. This classic Latin dish is one of my greatest hits. *Ropa vieja* is made all up and down the Caribbean. It means "old clothes" because of the look of the shredded beef that is tenderly, slowly infused with spices. My *abuelita* (grandmother) used to make this dish all the time, and the smell of *ropa vieja* simmering away always reminds me of summers in Puerto Rico.

For this dish I use one of my favorite pieces of kitchen equipment again, the slow cooker, an essential for busy working parents. You just throw it all in and simmer for 8 hours. It's a real people-pleaser that freezes well and makes even better leftovers. I like to make beef tacos or burritos the next day.

To eat this dish the traditional way, serve it up with Classic Brazilian Black Beans & Rice (page 220).

1. Season the flank steak with Sazón, then put the meat into a slow cooker. Layer the onion and bell peppers on top. Add the crushed tomatoes, broth, tomato paste, vinegar, garlic, oregano, and cumin, stirring to combine.

2. Pour in the beer and a splash of Tabasco, if desired. Spoon and stir the seasoned liquids over the beef and vegetables. Cover and cook on Low for 8 hours or High for 4 hours. Toward the last hour, add the olives (if using).

3. When done, shred the beef using two forks. Top with cilantro and serve.

[SLOW COOKER ROPA VIEJA WITH CLASSIC

BRAZILIAN BLACK BEANS & RICE]

PICADINHO
(Brazilian Ground Beef with Vegetables)

GLUTEN-FREE
SERVES 8

3 tablespoons extra-virgin olive oil

1 large white onion, chopped

2 garlic cloves, minced

2 pounds lean ground beef

1 (14-ounce) can diced tomatoes
with juices

½ cup chopped fresh parsley

4 large eggs

Pinch of red pepper flakes

Salt and freshly ground black pepper

1 medium russet potato, peeled
and cut into small cubes

2 celery stalks, chopped

1 red bell pepper, chopped

1 cup dry red wine

1 cup beef broth

Note: This recipes takes
about 20 minutes to prep and
1½ hours to cook.

GROUND BEEF CAN BE SO BORING, but not when made this way. (And I'm happy when my kids are getting plenty of nutrients and veggies, but with no complaints!) Growing up, my mom would make this Brazilian classic pretty much once a week because it's so good, quick, and easy—not to mention, budget friendly. *Picadinho*—pronounced *pi-ca-DEE-nyo*—is like a Brazilian chili, typically served on top of white rice.

1. In a large skillet, heat the olive oil over medium heat. Add the onion and cook, stirring frequently so that they don't burn, until caramelized to a golden brown, about 10 minutes. Add the garlic in the last minute of cooking.

2. In a large bowl, stir together the ground beef, tomatoes with their juices, parsley, eggs, red pepper flakes, and a dash of salt and black pepper. Mix as if you were making a meat loaf.

3. Add the meat mixture to the skillet with the onion and garlic and cook over medium-high heat to brown the meat, breaking it up with a wooden spoon as it cooks, 5 to 7 minutes.

4. Stir in the potato, celery, bell pepper, wine, and broth. Cover and cook over medium-low heat for about 1 hour, stirring occasionally, until the liquid reduces and the potatoes are cooked. Season with salt and black pepper and serve.

BEEF CHURRASCO
(Brazilian-Style Kebabs)

GLUTEN-FREE
SERVES 4 TO 6

½ cup fresh orange juice

½ cup extra-virgin olive oil

½ cup minced white onion

⅓ cup fresh lemon juice

3 garlic cloves, minced

2 teaspoons Worcestershire sauce

2 teaspoons minced fresh oregano

1 teaspoon kosher salt

½ teaspoon freshly ground black pepper

Pinch of red pepper flakes

1½ pounds skirt steak

Red Pepper Steak Sauce (recipe follows)

Note: This recipe requires overnight marinating.

IN BRAZIL AND ARGENTINA, this is the most popular and flavorful way to grill meat. *Churrasco* typically starts with a good cut of skirt steak, which is more tender than flank steak, and a citrusy marinade. I like to prepare the meat and let it marinate overnight to ensure it soaks up all the flavor of the marinade. And to truly get the best *churrasco* flavor, make this on the grill over very hot coals or medium-high heat to get the right charring on the outside.

This is definitely on my short list for barbecues, when we have lots of people over, because it is so low maintenance. I prep it the day before, then just grill it 30 minutes before serving. Serve it with a chimichurri (see page 131) or the Red Pepper Steak Sauce I make here drizzled on top.

1. In a large glass (or other nonreactive) bowl, whisk together the orange juice, olive oil, onion, lemon juice, garlic, Worcestershire, oregano, salt, black pepper, and red pepper flakes. Pierce the skirt steak with a fork all over. Submerge the meat in the marinade, making sure it covers the meat entirely. Cover the bowl with plastic wrap or pour all the marinade and meat into a large plastic bag and refrigerate overnight.

2. Heat a grill to medium-high or, if you are using charcoal, let the coals become white. Place the meat on the grill and sear it on both sides to your liking—rare to medium, 8 to 10 minutes, respectively, is preferable for this cut.

3. Remove the meat and let it rest, covered with aluminum foil to preserve the heat, for 8 minutes. Slice thinly across the grain, and serve drizzled with Red Pepper Steak Sauce.

RED PEPPER STEAK SAUCE

2 large red bell peppers

¼ cup extra-virgin olive oil

1 small shallot, chopped

1 jalapeño, seeded and minced

1 small garlic clove, minced

1 teaspoon minced fresh oregano

Pinch of red pepper flakes

½ cup vegetable broth

Salt

1. Over an open gas flame, roast the red bell peppers until the skins are blackened—or preheat the oven to 400°F and roast the peppers until charred and soft, about 35 minutes. Put the charred peppers in a plastic bag to allow them to sweat for 10 minutes, which allows you to easily remove the blackened skin.

2. Peel off the skin, then remove the seeds and stems. Chop the peppers.

3. In a medium saucepan, heat the olive oil over medium heat. Add the shallot and cook, stirring, until translucent, about 3 minutes. Add the chopped roasted peppers, jalapeño, garlic, oregano, and red pepper flakes and cook, stirring, until the garlic is fragrant, 2 minutes more.

4. Pour in the broth, bring it to boil, then reduce the heat to maintain a simmer. Let the sauce reduce by about one-quarter. Transfer the sauce to a food processor, let cool briefly, and process until smooth. Season with salt. Refrigerate until ready to use. Any unused steak sauce can be kept in an airtight container in the refrigerator for up to 1 week. The sauce can be used hot or room temperature.

STEAK FAJITAS

GLUTEN-FREE
SERVES 4 TO 6

½ cup chopped fresh cilantro,
plus more for garnish

2 jalapeños, seeded and diced

Grated zest of 1 lime

Juice of 2 limes

6 tablespoons extra-virgin olive oil

4 garlic cloves, minced

2 tablespoons
Worcestershire sauce

2 teaspoons chili powder

1 teaspoon ground cumin

¾ teaspoon kosher salt

¼ teaspoon freshly ground
black pepper

2 pounds skirt or flank steak

1 large yellow onion,
halved and sliced

1 red bell pepper,
cut into ¼-inch-thick strips

1 green bell pepper, cut into
¼-inch-thick strips

2 cups sliced cremini or white
mushrooms

YOU CAN NEVER GO WRONG WITH FAJITAS, another great way to entertain large groups, especially steak fajitas, although this marinade works well with chicken, too. Allow the meat to marinate for a few hours if you can, for the best result.

Serve with warmed corn or flour tortillas and plenty of sides like Spanish rice, beans, grated cheese, guacamole, chopped lettuce, sour cream, and pico del gallo. Let everyone pile it all on and make their own.

1. In a medium bowl, whisk together the cilantro, jalapeños, lime zest, lime juice, 4 tablespoons of the olive oil, the garlic, Worcestershire, chili powder, cumin, salt, and black pepper. Reserve ½ cup of the marinade in a glass jar.

2. Using a fork, prick the meat all over, then add the steak to the marinade and turn to coat completely. Cover and refrigerate for at least 8 hours or preferably overnight.

3. In a large cast-iron skillet, heat the remaining 2 tablespoons olive oil over medium-high heat. Add the onion and cook, stirring, until it softens a bit, about 3 minutes. Add the bell peppers and mushrooms and cook, stirring, until softened, 5 minutes more. Stir in 2 tablespoons of the reserved marinade until warmed through, about 30 seconds. Set the vegetables aside.

4. In the same skillet (or on a preheated grill), cook the meat over medium-high heat for 4 minutes on each side for medium doneness. Remove the meat, cover with aluminum foil, and let it rest for 8 to 10 minutes.

recipe continues

5. In the same pan you cooked the vegetables in, heat the remainder of the reserved marinade over medium-high heat and simmer until it has reduced some, 4 to 5 minutes.

6. Slice the steak into fajita strips—thinly across the grain. Serve on a large platter with the onion, peppers, and mushrooms and drizzle all with the hot fajita sauce. Garnish with chopped cilantro.

Note: This dish requires a minimum of 8 hours marinating time.

CHINESE STEAK STIR-FRY with Peppers & Broccoli

SERVES 4

1 pound flank or sirloin beef, thinly sliced (¼ inch thick)

2 tablespoons cornstarch

2 tablespoons toasted sesame oil

1 tablespoon minced garlic

½ teaspoon grated fresh ginger

¼ cup low-sodium soy sauce

2 tablespoons dark brown sugar

1 tablespoon rice vinegar

¼ cup vegetable oil

1 cup coarsely chopped red bell pepper

1 cup coarsely chopped green bell pepper

1 cup broccoli florets (optional)

2 green onions, sliced

NO NEED FOR TAKEOUT with this easy and healthier at-home version of delicious Chinese stir-fry. From beginning to end, this recipe takes no more than 30 minutes, so it's a perfect low-stress weeknight winner. Use any tender cut of steak—flank, sirloin, or even filet—and slice it thinly before cooking. If you want to add more veggies, I like to add a cup of broccoli florets for an even more nutritious and delicious meal. Serve over white or brown rice.

1. Coat the beef slices evenly with the cornstarch.

2. Heat a small saucepan over medium heat. Add the sesame oil and then the garlic and ginger and cook, stirring, until fragrant, just a few seconds. Add the soy sauce, ¼ cup water, the brown sugar, and the vinegar. Whisk until the sauce thickens a bit, 4 to 5 minutes. Remove from the heat.

3. In a wok or large skillet, warm the vegetable oil over medium-high heat, then add the beef and cook, stirring continuously, until all pieces are browned. Transfer the beef to a plate.

4. In the same wok or large skillet, cook the bell peppers and broccoli (if using), stirring, until crisp-tender, about 3 minutes.

5. Return the beef to the wok with the vegetables. Add the green onions and pour the sauce over all. Cook for about 2 minutes more. Serve immediately.

BEEF PAPRIKASH
(Hungarian Goulash) with Egg Noodles

SERVES 4 TO 6

½ cup ketchup

¼ cup dark brown sugar

3 tablespoons Worcestershire sauce

1 tablespoon smoked paprika

1 teaspoon Dijon mustard

Pinch of cayenne pepper

¼ cup plus 2 tablespoons all-purpose flour

1½ pounds top sirloin beef or chuck, cut into cubes

Salt and freshly ground black pepper

2 tablespoons salted butter

½ cup chopped green bell pepper

1 medium yellow onion, cut in half, then sliced

2 garlic cloves, minced

2 cups beef broth

1 (12-ounce) package egg noodles

Sour cream, for serving

Chopped fresh parsley, for garnish

Note: You can easily make this dish in a slow cooker. Brown the meat a little first, along with the onion, peppers, and garlic. Then add the beef and the remaining ingredients and let it simmer on Low, covered, for about 6 hours.

ANOTHER DISH STRAIGHT FROM MY MOM, this is something of a variation on the stroganoff (page 133). The main difference is we remove the yogurt and mushrooms, but add plenty of delicious smoked paprika, along with ketchup, brown sugar, and a few other spices.

1. In a medium bowl, whisk together the ketchup, brown sugar, Worcestershire, paprika, mustard, and cayenne and set aside.

2. Put ¼ cup of the flour on a plate for dredging. Season the beef with salt and black pepper, then dredge it in the flour, shaking off the excess.

3. In a Dutch oven, melt the butter over medium heat. Add the meat and cook until browned on all sides, about 5 minutes. Add the bell pepper, onion and garlic and cook, stirring occasionally, until the onion starts to soften, 2 minutes more.

4. Pour the ketchup mixture over the meat and then stir in the broth. Reduce the heat to low, cover, and simmer until the meat is tender, about 2 hours.

5. During the last 20 minutes of cooking, bring a large pot of salted water to a boil. Cook the egg noodles according to the package directions.

5. In a small bowl, whisk the remaining 2 tablespoons flour with ¼ cup water to create a slurry. Stir it into the goulash and cook until the sauce has thickened up, about 2 minutes.

6. Serve the goulash on top of egg noodles with a dollop of sour cream, garnished with fresh parsley.

GRILLED CHIMICHURRI SOY STEAK

SERVES 6 TO 8

MARINADE

1 tablespoon low-sodium soy sauce

1 tablespoon toasted sesame oil

1 tablespoon rice vinegar

1 tablespoon dark brown sugar

1 teaspoon smoked paprika

1 garlic clove, minced

Pinch of freshly ground black pepper

3 pounds flank steak

CHIMICHURRI

2 cups chopped fresh parsley

1 cup chopped fresh cilantro

⅓ cup chopped red bell pepper

2 garlic cloves

½ cup extra-virgin olive oil

¼ cup red wine vinegar or sherry vinegar

1 teaspoon minced fresh oregano

½ teaspoon salt

Pinch of granulated sugar

Pinch of red pepper flakes

Nonstick cooking spray

I HAVE LEARNED YOU CAN PRETTY MUCH MAKE ANYTHING ON THE GRILL, and it will always taste better, even dessert. Grilling brings all the juices and flavors to the surface no matter what it is you are making, and it's an easier, faster, and a healthier way to cook. We grill almost every day of the week, and one of my biggest hits with kids and guests is this Chimichurri Soy Steak. For an easy complete meal, grilled vegetables are a good complement and taste amazing with a little chimichurri, as well.

1. **Make the marinade:** In a small bowl, mix the soy sauce, sesame oil, rice vinegar, brown sugar, paprika, garlic, and black pepper, forming a paste. Coat the flank steak with the paste and put it in a resealable plastic bag. Marinate in the refrigerator for 2 to 4 hours.

2. **Make the chimichurri:** In a blender or food processor, combine the parsley, cilantro, bell pepper, garlic, olive oil, red wine vinegar, oregano, salt, granulated sugar, and red pepper flakes and lightly pulse until combined and no longer chunky, but not completely pureed.

3. Remove the marinated meat from the refrigerator and allow it to come to room temperature.

4. Heat a grill (charcoal or gas) to medium and spray with nonstick spray.

recipe continues

5. Grill the steak, covered, for 7 to 10 minutes on each side for medium-rare (a bit less if you like it more rare).

6. Remove the steak from the grill and let it rest, covered with aluminum foil, for 10 minutes to allow the juices to settle and the temperature to even. On a cutting board, thinly slice the steak across the grain. Liberally drizzle the slices with the chimichurri sauce and serve.

Note: This dish requires a minimum of 2 hours marinating time.

BEEF STROGANOFF

Salt

2 cups beef broth

½ cup plain full-fat Greek yogurt or sour cream, plus more for garnish

2 tablespoons Worcestershire sauce

¼ cup plus 2 tablespoons all-purpose flour

1½ pounds sirloin steak, cut into thin strips

Freshly ground black pepper

3 tablespoons unsalted butter

1 pound baby bella or cremini mushrooms, sliced ⅛ inch thick

1 cup sliced yellow onion (cut in half, then into thin slices)

2 garlic cloves, minced

1 (12-ounce) package egg noodles

½ cup dry white wine

Chopped fresh parsley, for garnish

IF YOU LOVE BEEF AND MUSHROOMS TOGETHER, this is a hearty, wholesome dinner that goes deliciously over rice or egg noodles. Stroganoff is such a nostalgic recipe for me, as my mom would make this on chilly nights or when we needed some comfort food. Her version uses cream of mushroom soup, which is really, really good, but perhaps a little too rich for my blood. So, using her recipe as my inspiration, I reworked it, and it's even yummier, a bit healthier, and takes only 30 minutes to make. And while mushrooms used to scare my kids off, I will say Josh has come around and really enjoys them now; he actually eats up all the mushrooms first, then works his way to the beef. Luke, well, he's a work in progress, but he does love the beef and the stroganoff sauce.

1. Bring a large pot of salted water to a boil.

2. In a large bowl, whisk together the broth, yogurt, Worcestershire, and 2 tablespoons of the flour and set aside. Put the remaining flour on a plate for dredging.

3. Season the steak strips with salt and pepper, then dredge them in the flour, coating the steak evenly and shaking off any excess.

4. In a large skillet, melt 2 tablespoons of the butter over medium-high heat. When bubbling, add the steak and cook, stirring occasionally, until lightly browned on all sides, about 6 minutes total. Remove the steak and set aside.

recipe continues

5. Melt the remaining 1 tablespoon butter in the pan and stir in the mushrooms, onion, and garlic. Season with salt and pepper. Cook, stirring frequently, until the mushrooms release their liquids and the onion begins to soften, about 5 minutes.

6. Meanwhile, cook the egg noodles in the pot of boiling water according to the package directions.

7. Stir the wine into the mushroom mixture, letting it cook down for about 3 minutes. Pour in the yogurt sauce and return the beef to the pan. Bring to a simmer and cook until the sauce is evenly incorporated and the stroganoff is creamy, about 3 minutes.

8. Serve on top of the egg noodles, garnished with a dollop of yogurt and chopped fresh parsley.

CHATEAUBRIAND BAKED IN A SALT-HERB CRUST

SERVES 10 TO 12

4 large egg whites

2 cups salt

2 tablespoons freshly ground black pepper

¼ cup chopped fresh rosemary (leaves and stems), or 1 tablespoon dried

¼ cup chopped fresh parsley, or 1 tablespoon dried

¼ cup chopped fresh thyme (leaves and stems), or 1 tablespoon dried

¼ cup chopped fresh sage, or 1 tablespoon dried

4 cups all-purpose flour, plus more if needed

1 tablespoon extra-virgin olive oil

1 (5- to 6-pound) whole beef tenderloin (chateaubriand-style), trimmed of fat

1 large egg yolk, mixed with 1 tablespoon water to make an egg wash

AN IMPRESSIVE DINNER that will really wow anyone you serve it to, I save this dish for really special guests or events. While it sounds complicated and very "gourmet," I can assure you it's about the easiest thing you will ever make, and no one needs to know your secret! It is a luxury meal, as the beef should be a really great cut of tenderloin, but you will have no regrets as you hear your guests *ooh* and *ahh* over your "talents." Keep the rest of the meal simple and present the beef baked in the crust at the table. Your company will be blown away by the wafting aroma as you present the most tender and juicy beef tenderloin, cooked to perfection. Just do not eat the crust, as it will be way too salty! It falls away easily as you carve the meat.

1. In a large bowl, whisk the egg whites with 1 cup water, the salt, and pepper. Then stir in the rosemary, parsley, thyme, and sage. Mix the flour in a little at a time to make sure the herbs are evenly blended into the dough. The dough should be like a bread dough if you knead it by hand. It shouldn't be too sticky or tacky. Adjust the flour accordingly. Cover the dough and set aside at room temperature for at least 2 hours. Or refrigerate overnight covered in plastic to use the next day. Be sure to let the dough come back to room temperature, though, before rolling it out.

2. Preheat the oven to 400°F. Line a large baking dish with parchment paper.

recipe continues

Notes: Remove the meat from the refrigerator about 30 minutes before cooking to ensure proper timing. • For an even easier recipe, you can use store-bought dough and knead in the salt, pepper, and herbs.

3. In a cast-iron skillet, heat the olive oil over high heat. Add the tenderloin and sear, rotating it as needed until it has a nice crust on all sides, about 5 minutes total. Remove from the skillet and allow to cool for 10 to 15 minutes.

4. On a floured surface, roll out the dough to a roughly ¼-inch-thick rectangular shape, large enough to fit and wrap the beef entirely. (Since it's so large, I find it easiest to roll it out right on the parchment, then lift the rolled dough onto the pan.)

5. Set the dough in the prepared baking dish. Put the beef in the middle and cover it, wrapping it like a baby in a blanket or folding an envelope; cut away any excess dough. Seal the top seams with the egg wash. And fold the sides under the beef or press the ends together. Brush the top with the remaining egg wash.

6. Roast to your preferred level of doneness, 25 to 30 minutes. Remove from the oven and test the beef by inserting a meat thermometer. For rare, the temperature should be 120 to 125°F; medium should be 130 to 135°F. When you remove it from the oven, the beef will continue to cook internally, rising perhaps another 10 degrees while resting for about 15 minutes, so take that into account as well. Serve tableside.

PERFECT BEEF FILET
with Herbed Butter

HERBED BUTTER

½ cup (1 stick) unsalted butter, at room temperature or softened in the microwave for 15 seconds

1 garlic clove, minced

1½ teaspoons fresh thyme leaves

1½ teaspoons minced fresh chives

1 teaspoon minced fresh tarragon

1 teaspoon minced fresh oregano

1 teaspoon finely chopped fresh rosemary

Salt and freshly ground black pepper

FILET

1½ pounds filet mignon, sliced into 4 pieces, each 1½ inches thick

1 tablespoon extra-virgin olive oil

1 teaspoon coarse sea salt

½ teaspoon freshly ground black pepper

THIS IS THE MOST DELICIOUS FILET YOU WILL EVER HAVE, better than any steakhouse. Just make sure you have really fresh filet mignon to start, and the rest is easy. My kids devour filet, but especially love the flavors the herbed butter imparts. It's a great dinner when you have company over as well, as it is sure to impress and very low maintenance to make. Use any leftover butter for delicious French bread or pour it over steamed vegetables to serve along with the steak.

1. **Make the herbed butter:** An hour (or more) prior to cooking the beef, in the bowl of a stand mixer (or in a large bowl using a hand mixer), beat together the butter, garlic, thyme, chives, tarragon, oregano, and rosemary. Season with salt and pepper and mix thoroughly once more.

2. Drop the butter into the middle of a sheet of plastic wrap or waxed paper, form it into an oval cylinder like a candy, and twist the ends. Refrigerate for at least an hour.

3. **Cook the filets:** Preheat the oven to 400°F. Bring the filets to room temperature (take them out of the refrigerator about 30 minutes beforehand).

4. In an oven-safe or cast-iron skillet, melt 1 tablespoon of the herbed butter with the olive oil over high heat.

5. Season the filets with the salt and pepper, then sear the meat on the skillet, about 3 minutes on each side.

6. Move the skillet to the oven and cook to the preferred doneness, about 6 minutes for medium-rare, 8 minutes for medium, and 9 to 10 minutes for medium-well to well-done.

7. Let the steak rest for 5 minutes, covered with aluminum foil to preserve the heat. Top each filet with a pat of the herbed butter right before serving.

PORK

SWEET-&-SOUR PORK & VEGETABLES

SAUCE

2 tablespoons fresh orange juice

2 tablespoons apple cider vinegar

2 tablespoons ketchup

2 tablespoons dark brown sugar

1 tablespoon pineapple juice

1 tablespoon low-sodium soy sauce

1 tablespoon cornstarch

STIR-FRY

¼ cup cornstarch

¼ cup all-purpose flour

2 large eggs, beaten

1 pound boneless pork loin,
cut into 1-inch cubes

3 tablespoons vegetable oil or canola oil

½ cup coarsely chopped yellow onion

½ red bell pepper, cut into ¾-inch pieces

½ green bell pepper, cut into ¾-inch pieces

2 garlic cloves, minced

1 teaspoon grated fresh ginger

1 cup pineapple chunks
(can be frozen or canned)

BETTER THAN TAKEOUT and way healthier, too. My kids love that this dish is a bit tangy and sweet at the same time. You can make this with chicken, if you prefer, but there is nothing like the Chinese classic, pork. While most sweet-and-sour recipes call for deep-frying the pork in oil first, I prefer to lightly stir-fry it instead, removing some of the fat and calories.

Enjoy with a side of steamed white or brown rice—though my kids love white sticky rice.

1. **Make the sauce:** In a saucepan, whisk together ¼ cup water, the orange juice, vinegar, ketchup, brown sugar, pineapple juice, soy sauce, and cornstarch. Bring to a simmer over medium heat and cook, stirring continuously, until the sauce thickens and reduces, about 5 minutes. Reduce the heat to low and keep warm until ready to use.

2. **Make the stir-fry:** In a bowl, mix the cornstarch, flour, and eggs. If the batter is too thick to coat the pork, add 1 to 2 tablespoons water. Toss the pork in the batter to coat evenly.

3. In a wok, heat the vegetable oil over medium heat. Add the pork and cook, stirring, until golden brown and cooked through, 3 to 5 minutes, then remove and drain on paper towels. Remove any excess batter from the wok.

4. With the wok over medium-high heat, cook the onion, bell peppers, garlic, and ginger, stirring, until they are a bit tender, 2 to 3 minutes. Return the pork to the wok and gently stir in the pineapple chunks.

5. Pour the sauce into the wok and cook to allow the pork to absorb sauce, 2 minutes more. Serve with a side of steamed rice.

PORK CHOPS
in an Apple-Fig Balsamic Reduction

GLUTEN-FREE
SERVES 4

1½ pounds bone-in pork chops
(4 or 5 chops, about ½ inch thick)

Salt and freshly ground black pepper

1 cup apple cider

5 medium fresh or dried figs, quartered

2 garlic cloves, minced

1 tablespoon balsamic vinegar

1 teaspoon fresh thyme leaves

2 shallots, thinly sliced

A HEARTY FALL MEAL, with apples and figs, is so homey, and I also like that you can just eat the pork off the bone—just delicious. My kids appreciate that it has a little bit of that sweet-tooth satisfaction. And it's so fast—you can make it in 30 minutes.

1. Preheat the oven to 400°F.

2. Put the pork chops in a large baking dish and season the chops with salt and pepper.

3. In a small saucepan, mix the cider, figs, garlic, vinegar, thyme, and a pinch each of salt and pepper. Bring to a boil over medium-high heat, then reduce the heat to medium-low and simmer until the sauce has reduced by half, about 12 minutes. Mush the figs a bit into the sauce.

4. Pour the sauce over the pork chops and sprinkle the shallots over the top. Bake for about 10 minutes, then flip on the other side and bake for 5 minutes more. Spoon the pan sauce over the pork chops and serve immediately.

GRILLED HONEY DIJON PORK TENDERLOIN
with Baby New Potatoes & Green Beans

SERVES 4 TO 6

MARINADE

⅔ cup extra-virgin olive oil

¼ cup fresh lemon juice

2 tablespoons whole-grain Dijon mustard

1 tablespoon honey

1 green onion, thinly sliced

1 garlic clove, minced

1 teaspoon minced fresh thyme,
or ¼ teaspoon dried

1 teaspoon minced fresh oregano,
or ¼ teaspoon dried

1 teaspoon minced fresh rosemary,
or ¼ teaspoon dried

½ teaspoon grated lemon zest

½ teaspoon salt

½ teaspoon freshly ground black pepper

PORK

2 pounds pork tenderloin

Salt and freshly ground black pepper

1 pound fresh French green beans,
washed and trimmed

2 cups halved baby red potatoes

3 green onions, cut lengthwise
into thin ribbons

THIS IS A LOW-FUSS MEAL you can make in about 30 minutes, though I do recommend letting the pork marinate for the deepest flavor and tenderness. It's a good one for when you have company over, as you can prep it all before your guests arrive, then throw the tenderloin on the grill and the potatoes and green bean foil packs either in the oven or on the grill, and that's all!

1. **Make the marinade:** In a medium bowl, whisk together the olive oil, lemon juice, mustard, honey, green onion, garlic, thyme, oregano, rosemary, lemon zest, salt, and pepper. Set aside in the refrigerator. Bring to room temperature and whisk again before using.

2. **Marinate the pork:** Season the pork with salt and pepper and place in a large resealable plastic bag. Add three-quarters of the marinade (reserving the last quarter for the green beans and potatoes) and marinate the pork in the refrigerator for 1 hour.

3. Heat a grill to medium-high, about 400°F. Preheat the oven to 450°F (if you're using the oven method for the vegetables).

4. Put the beans and potatoes in a covered microwavable dish with 2 tablespoons water. Microwave on high for 2 minutes. Remove and let sit until cool, with the lid still on, to allow them to steam. Drain any liquid out of the dish.

5. **Assemble the veggie packets:** Place the green beans, potatoes, and green onions in the center of a large piece (about 18 by 28 inches) of heavy-duty aluminum foil, enough to bring up the sides and create a foil packet around the vegetables. (It helps to

recipe continues

Notes: I like to use very thin French greens beans or haricots verts, but if you can't find them you can make French-style green beans by trimming regular green beans, then slicing in half lengthwise. • Allow 1 hour to marinate prior to grilling. You can use either the grill or the oven for the vegetable packets.

put the foil into a 2-inch deep baking dish, put the veggies in, and fold the overhanging foil up over the veggies to make the packet.) Drizzle the remaining marinade over the vegetables, season with a pinch of salt and pepper, then seal the packet closed. Put the packet directly on the preheated grill. Grill for 30 minutes.

To oven bake the veggie packets: Assemble the packets as per Step 4. Put the packet into the preheated oven, directly on the oven rack, and bake until the vegetables are cooked, 30 to 35 minutes. Open up the packet after 30 minutes and check for doneness. Put it back into the oven and cook with packet open for the last 5 minutes.

6. Remove the pork tenderloin from the marinade and put it on the grill. Rotate to cook on all sides, basting with the marinade from the bag occasionally using a grill brush. For medium-well, the pork will be done in about 35 minutes, though once off the grill check the temperature to make sure it registers about 145°F internally. Let it rest for 5 minutes, then slice.

7. Put the foil packet of vegetables in a deep serving platter, open it, remove the foil, and arrange the sliced pork on top of the vegetables. Serve.

PERNIL
(Roast Pork Shoulder)

1 (6- to 8-pound) whole pork shoulder (butt), with fat on

MARINADE
8 garlic cloves, crushed

¼ cup white wine vinegar or red wine vinegar

¼ cup extra-virgin olive oil

3 tablespoons fresh oregano, or 2 teaspoons dried

1 tablespoon smoked paprika

1 tablespoon salt

2 teaspoons freshly ground black pepper

GRAVY
2 tablespoons all-purpose flour

2 tablespoons unsalted butter, at room temperature

1 cup dry white wine

Salt and freshly ground black pepper

PERNIL (*PRONOUNCED* *PARE-KNEEL*) is a real Latin tradition during the holidays. Instead of turkey, this is often the centerpiece along with *arroz con gandules* (rice and pigeon peas). When I think about it, I can still taste the *pernil* after spending a holiday with my grandparents in Puerto Rico. Like a turkey, it's served with gravy and, depending on the size of the pork shoulder, you can feed at least eight to ten people. And pork always makes for the most delicious leftovers: pork sandwiches, burritos, or tacos, or served on top of pasta.

This recipe needs a little tender loving care, but it really is fairly easy and hands off. You just need time to allow the meat to marinate overnight and then roast for several hours, but when done it should just fall off the bone and melt in your mouth.

1. Score the fat on the pork shoulder with a sharp knife, cutting a diamond pattern. Don't cut into the pork itself.

2. **Make the marinade:** In a bowl, mix together the garlic, vinegar, olive oil, oregano, paprika, salt, and pepper. Rub it liberally into the pork (rubber gloves help), getting it into the slits in the fat and on all sides. Cover the pork and marinate in the refrigerator overnight.

3. Remove the pork from the refrigerator about 1 hour before cooking so it can come to room temperature, which allows it to roast more evenly.

4. Preheat the oven to 325°F.

recipe continues

5. Place the pork in a roasting pan on a rack (like you would a turkey) with the fat-side down. Pour 4 cups water into the pan, then roast for 1 hour. Flip the pork so the scored fat is face up and roast for 4½ hours more. Occasionally baste the top with the drippings in the pan. It is done when the outside is a beautiful crispy brown and the internal temperature reads about 175°F.

6. Remove from the oven and tent with aluminum foil. Let it rest for 15 to 20 minutes before carving. When cooled enough, cut around the T-shaped bone and remove it. Carve thinly with a serrated knife, as you would a ham or turkey.

7. **Make the gravy:** Pour the pork drippings from the pan into a separator, to remove most of the fat, or large spouted measuring cup. In a separate measuring cup, mix the flour and butter, then add the drippings, using a fork mash it into a thick paste. In a saucepan, heat the white wine and ½ cup water over medium heat. Pour the paste into the saucepan and whisk until the gravy thickens, 5 to 8 minutes. Season with salt and pepper. Serve alongside the pernil roast.

SWEET-&-SPICY SLOW-ROASTED PULLED PORK

SERVES 10 TO 12

BRINE

2 cups distilled white vinegar

½ cup salt

1 tablespoon whole black peppercorns

1 tablespoon mustard powder

¼ cup packed dark brown sugar

2 bay leaves

1 (5-pound) pork shoulder (butt), preferably bone-in

DRY RUB

¼ cup packed dark brown sugar

1 tablespoon cayenne powder

1 tablespoon garlic powder

1 tablespoon sweet paprika

1 tablespoon chili powder

1 tablespoon onion powder

1 tablespoon ground cumin

HERE'S A SOLID FAMILY MEAL that's also useful for large gatherings. There is some advance planning involved to allow the pork to brine and then slow roast overnight. The great part about it is that once it's in the oven, it's lights out, and when you wake up in the morning you will have a fall-off-the bone delicious pulled pork. Serve on a fresh potato roll or by itself, with coleslaw or pickles.

1. **Make the brine:** In a large saucepan, combine 6 cups water, the white vinegar, salt, peppercorns, mustard, brown sugar, and bay leaves. Bring to a slow boil over medium heat, then remove from the heat. Allow to cool slightly.

2. Pour the brine into a 2-gallon resealable plastic bag or other large container and add the pork. Seal and brine in the refrigerator for at least 12 hours, though 24 is ideal.

3. **Make the dry rub:** In a medium bowl, stir together the brown sugar, cayenne, garlic powder, paprika, chili powder, onion powder, and cumin and set aside.

4. Preheat the oven to 225°F. (Yes it is very low and slow, but deliciously worth it.)

5. Remove the pork shoulder from the brine and dry it with paper towels. Reserving 3 tablespoons of the dry rub for the final sauce, coat the pork shoulder on all sides with the rub, working it into each nook and cranny. Set the pork shoulder in a large pan and roast it slowly overnight, 8 to 10 hours (roughly 2 hours per

pound). You will know it is done when you can shred a piece with just a fork or when the bone loosely pulls away.

6. Remove it from oven and, using two forks, shred the pork off the bone onto a platter.

7. Make the sauce: In a large pot or Dutch oven, heat the olive oil over medium heat. Add the onion, garlic, and tomato paste and cook, stirring continuously, for about 1 minute. Slowly pour in the apple cider vinegar and cook, stirring continuously, until the onion is softened, 2 to 3 minutes more. Stir in the ketchup, mustard, reserved 3 tablespoons dry rub, Worcestershire, and bay leaf, then the shredded pork. Simmer over low heat, stirring occasionally, until the sauce has thickened and the pork has soaked it up, 45 minutes to 1 hour. Remove the bay leaf and you're ready to serve.

Note: For the best results, I recommend starting this at least the day before, or better yet, 2 days before you plan to serve so that the pork is able to soak in the brine for at least 12 to 24 hours. Then it will take about 8 hours to roast overnight. (For example, start this on a Thursday or Friday night and on Saturday you can begin the slow roast to serve Sunday.) The effort up front is well worth it, I promise you.

SAUCE

1 tablespoon extra-virgin olive oil

1 large yellow onion, sliced

5 garlic cloves, minced

1 tablespoon tomato paste

¾ cup apple cider vinegar

⅓ cup ketchup

2 tablespoons Dijon mustard

2 teaspoons Worcestershire sauce

1 bay leaf

BARBECUED CHOPS

PORK CHOPS

¼ cup chopped fresh thyme
(leaves and stems)

2 tablespoons granulated sugar

2 tablespoons salt

6 (8- to 10-ounce) bone-in pork chops,
about 1 inch thick

BARBECUE SAUCE

2 tablespoons canola oil

½ Vidalia or sweet onion, chopped

½ teaspoon salt

¼ teaspoon freshly ground black pepper

3 garlic cloves, minced

½ cup ketchup

½ cup packed dark brown sugar

¼ cup apple cider vinegar

¼ cup honey

¼ cup coarse-grain Dijon mustard

1 teaspoon Worcestershire sauce

½ teaspoon cayenne pepper

2 tablespoons canola oil,
for cooking the pork

IN MY HOUSE, PORK IS THE "OTHER WHITE MEAT." In fact, Luke calls it chicken, and I don't correct him. What he doesn't know when it comes to eating can't hurt, and if he likes it and eats it, even better. These chops are finger-licking good because they are sweet and tangy, and usually they get rave reviews from the pickiest eaters. Yes, you can buy store-bought barbecue sauce and it is yummy, too, but this way I can control how much spice goes into the sauce, and I know what my kids will and won't eat. Also, if it helps, you can make the sauce a few days beforehand, then baste as you grill the chops and add more of the sauce at the end before serving. Add some fresh corn on the cob, a green salad, or coleslaw, and you have yourself a home-run dinner.

1. **Brine the pork chops:** In a glass baking dish, mix together 3 cups water, the thyme, granulated sugar, and salt and stir until the salt and sugar have dissolved. Brine the chops in the mixture, covered, in the refrigerator for about 30 minutes before grilling.

2. **Make the barbecue sauce:** In a saucepan, heat the canola oil over medium heat, then add the onion, salt, and pepper and cook, stirring, until the onion is soft, 3 to 5 minutes. Add the garlic and cook, stirring, until the garlic is fragrant, about 1 minute.

3. Add the ketchup, brown sugar, vinegar, honey, mustard, Worcestershire, and cayenne and stir well. Let the sauce simmer and thicken for about 15 minutes, then add water to thin it to the desired thickness, if necessary.

4. **Cook the chops:** Heat a grill to medium and brush each of the chops on both sides with the canola oil.

5. Grill the chops first without the sauce for about 2 minutes on each side, then baste on both sides with the barbecue sauce. Cook until you have a nice char and grill marks, 3 minutes more on each side, depending on your grill. Use an instant-read thermometer to test the meat; you're looking for an internal temperature of least 145°F. If they're not there yet, move the chops to a cooler part of the grill. Turn once again and baste both sides, allowing the chops to grill until done. Remove from the grill and tent with aluminum foil while you plate the meal.

Note: Unused barbecue sauce can be kept in a sealed container in the refrigerator for about a week.

WHOLE WHEAT SPAGHETTI CARBONARA

with Peas & Pancetta

SERVES 4

12 ounces whole wheat spaghetti (¾ box)

1 tablespoon extra-virgin olive oil

1 cup chopped pancetta

1 large shallot, minced
(about 3 tablespoons)

2 large eggs, room temperature

½ cup freshly grated Parmesan cheese

1 cup fresh or frozen green peas

Salt and freshly ground black pepper

THIS IS ONE OF OUR FAVORITE PASTA DISHES. It is so flavorful and easy to make that I make it in front of friends to impress them. You can use regular spaghetti, of course, but I like the nuttiness of whole wheat, and it's a bit healthier, too. From beginning to end, this spaghetti carbonara takes less than 30 minutes, so be ready to eat it right away, as it's best right out of the pan and onto your plate!

1. Line a plate with paper towels. Warm your serving bowl(s) in a low oven.

2. Bring a large pot of salted water to a boil. Cook the pasta according to the package directions to al dente.

3. As the pasta is cooking, in a nonstick skillet, heat the olive oil over medium heat. Add the pancetta and shallot and cook, stirring, until the pancetta has just become crispy and lightly browned, 4 to 5 minutes. Spoon the pancetta and shallot onto the paper towel–lined plate and set aside any rendered fat in a small bowl.

4. In a medium bowl, whisk the eggs with 3 tablespoons of the Parmesan. In a stream, whisking vigorously, add the rendered pancetta fat to the eggs.

5. When about a minute remains until the pasta is cooked, add the peas to the pasta water to heat them. Then reserve 1 cup of the pasta water for the sauce and drain the pasta and peas in a colander.

6. In the same pot you made the pasta, but off the burner so you don't cook the eggs, dump the spaghetti and peas back into the pot, then add the egg mixture, pancetta, and shallot. Toss continuously to prevent the eggs from clumping. Add the reserved pasta water, bit by bit as needed, to achieve a creamier texture. Season with salt and pepper.

7. Serve immediately, topping each warm bowl with a healthy spoonful of the remaining Parmesan.

FISH & SEAFOOD

CRISPY SHRIMP with Mango-Pineapple Soy Sauce

SERVES 4 TO 6

MANGO-PINEAPPLE SOY SAUCE

½ cup mango nectar (available in the Spanish section of the market)

¼ cup chopped fresh or frozen mango pieces

¼ cup chopped canned pineapple

1 tablespoon low-sodium soy sauce

½ teaspoon grated fresh ginger

Pinch of freshly ground black pepper

SHRIMP

1¼ cups all-purpose flour

1 tablespoon Old Bay seasoning

4 large egg whites, lightly beaten

2 cups panko or plain bread crumbs

1 teaspoon salt

30 large raw shrimp (about 1½ pounds), peeled, tails left on, and deveined

¼ cup extra-virgin olive oil, plus more as needed

IF I COULD EAT FISH MOST NIGHTS OF THE WEEK, I WOULD, and here in California I'm spoiled by an abundance of fresh seafood. I've been inspired to make it more often, trying out new recipes and flavor combinations on my favorite little picky taste-testers. White flaky fish, like cod and sole, seem to work best with my family, along with that most popular of shellfish, shrimp.

Here's another one of those Latin-Asian-inspired dishes that I love so much. The sweetness of pineapple and mango and the salty soy sauce are just the right combination for the crispy shrimp. Serve it as a meal with the coconut rice (page 222) and a vegetable on the side, or as an easy appetizer.

1. **Make the mango-pineapple soy sauce:** In a saucepan, combine the mango nectar, mango pieces, pineapple, soy sauce, ginger, and pepper and simmer gently until reduced by a quarter and slightly thickened, 4 to 5 minutes. Set aside.

2. Preheat the oven to 475°F.

3. **Make the shrimp:** In a shallow bowl, mix the flour with the Old Bay seasoning. In a second shallow bowl, beat the egg whites, and in a third shallow bowl, mix the bread crumbs and the salt.

4. First dredge the shrimp in the flour, then dip in the egg whites, letting any excess drip off, and then roll in the bread crumbs to coat.

recipe continues

Note: Prep the crispy shrimp ahead of time and cook it up quickly right before you're ready to serve.

5. Pour the olive oil into a large rimmed baking sheet or roasting pan and spread to coat the bottom. Press each shrimp in the oil, then turn to coat the other side, adding more oil to the pan if necessary to coat all of the shrimp. Set them slightly apart in pan. (For crispier shrimp and to cut down prep time, you can make the shrimp ahead to this point and leave uncovered in the refrigerator until ready to cook. The batter dries in the refrigerator just enough to make them a bit crispier.)

6. Transfer to the oven and bake the shrimp for 6 to 8 minutes, until golden brown on the bottom, then flip over and bake for 5 minutes more, until golden brown on the other side.

7. Serve immediately with the Mango-Pineapple Soy Sauce for dipping.

PESTO SHRIMP
with Lemon-Pepper Fettuccine & Peas

SERVES 4

1 teaspoon salt, plus more for seasoning

16 ounces dried fettuccine

½ cup Easy Pesto (recipe follows)

1½ pounds large fresh shrimp, peeled and deveined

1 (8-ounce) bag frozen peas, thawed

¼ cup fresh lemon juice

¼ cup freshly grated Parmesan cheese

1 tablespoon unsalted butter

Freshly ground black pepper

Grated zest of ½ lemon

Note: This is another family classic that you can make in 30 minutes, especially if you have some home-made pesto on hand. Freeze any leftover pesto sauce in a tightly sealed plastic bag or ice cube trays to always have it at the ready.

DURING OUR TRAVELS TO ITALY, along the Ligurian coast, my husband fell in love with Genovese pesto. An easy sauce that makes a very flavorful marinade, there's no reason not to make this flexible favorite fresh at home. I like to have a bunch of basil on hand at all times because it adds such brightness to just about any food. Here it adds a beautiful color and flavor to the shrimp, alongside zesty lemon fettuccine.

1. Bring about 4 quarts water to a boil in a large pasta pot. Add salt to the water. Add the fettuccine and cook according to the package instructions. Drain the pasta and return it to the pot.

2. In a skillet, warm the Easy Pesto over medium heat. Add the shrimp and cook, stirring, until just cooked through, 4 to 5 minutes each side. Stir in the peas until warmed, about 2 minutes.

3. To the pot with the fettuccine, add the lemon juice, Parmesan, butter, and pepper. Stir in the shrimp and peas. Season with salt and pepper.

4. Serve garnished with the lemon zest.

EASY PESTO

MAKES ABOUT
1½ CUPS

2 cups fresh basil leaves

3 tablespoons pine nuts

2 garlic cloves, chopped

½ cup extra-virgin olive oil

¼ cup freshly grated Parmesan cheese

Salt

GOT LEFTOVER PESTO? Try it on sandwiches, eggs, fish, shrimp, pork, and chicken, and, of course, any pasta in the pantry. Cover the pesto tightly with a layer of plastic wrap to keep the air out (so the pesto doesn't turn dark green), then close the container and refrigerate for up to a week.

In a food processor, combine the basil, pine nuts, and garlic and process until finely chopped. Add the olive oil in a thin stream, blending until incorporated. Add the Parmesan and blend until smooth. Season with salt.

BAHIAN COD FILLET with Coconut Milk, Peppers & Onions

GLUTEN FREE
SERVES 4 TO 6

4 fillets cod (about 1½ pounds)

Juice of 1 lime

Salt and freshly ground black pepper

2 tablespoons extra-virgin olive oil

1 cup thinly sliced yellow onion

2 garlic cloves, minced

½ red bell pepper, thinly sliced

½ green bell pepper, thinly sliced

2 tablespoons tomato paste

2 teaspoons sweet paprika

½ teaspoon ground turmeric

1 (14-ounce) can coconut milk

Pinch of red pepper flakes (or more, if you prefer more heat)

1 cup chopped fresh cilantro

I MADE THIS DISH for the *TODAY* show. In its traditional form, it's called *moqueca* (pronounced *moh-KEH-kah*). It's a typical seafood stew from Bahia, along the northeast coastline of Brazil, where they like to cook with coconut milk and flavor foods with native fruits, like passion fruit and mango.

While *moqueca* is a little more complex, as it uses dende oil or palm oil, which may be harder to find (I did find it on Amazon), I simplified the recipe using only easy-to-find ingredients and just one type of fish (either cod or firm white halibut work best).

Serve the fish on a bed of white rice or my Coconut Rice (page 222).

1. Pat the fish dry with paper towels and put the fillets in a large glass bowl. Season with the lime juice and salt and black pepper to taste and set aside.

2. In a Dutch oven, heat the olive oil over medium heat. Add the onion and garlic and cook, stirring, until the onion begins to soften, 2 to 3 minutes.

3. Add the bell peppers, tomato paste, paprika, and turmeric, mixing well. Cook, stirring, until the bell peppers begin to soften, about 4 minutes.

4. Lay the fish fillets on top of the vegetables and pour in the coconut milk. Cover the pot and lower the heat to medium-low. Cook until the fish is just cooked through, about 15 minutes.

5. Season with salt and black pepper, a pinch (or more) of red pepper flakes, and the fresh cilantro right before serving.

GREEK GRILLED FISH

GLUTEN FREE
SERVES 4

¼ cup plus 3 tablespoons
extra-virgin olive oil

4 whole branzino or striped bass
(about 4 pounds total)

4 sprigs fresh thyme

4 sprigs fresh rosemary

2 tablespoons chopped fresh oregano

1 fennel bulb, stalks and bulb cut up into
very thin rounds

1 bunch fresh parsley

1 lemon, halved

Salt and freshly ground black pepper

Note: Have your fish market scale
and gut the fish for you.

ONE OF MY FAVORITE MEMORIES from the Summer Olympics in Athens in 2004 was going to the port along with my work friends and eating at one of the typical Greek outdoor portside restaurants. The fish was fresh every day, and they would present the platter to you and let you pick your fish. They'd then take it back and season it just with fresh herbs and the most amazing olive oil, then bake it or grill it, and present it to the table whole (which can take some getting used to if you are not into seeing the whole head and soulless eyes). Then they bone the fish and cut out the white flaky fillets, drizzling them with more fresh olive oil and lemon juice. No fish has ever tasted better, in my opinion.

Well, I try to replicate at least the seasonings and flavor at home, and using the freshest branzino or loup de mer, which is a European sea bass. You can use any type of white bass or striped bass instead. And best to cook it whole, as it makes it next to impossible to overcook or dry it out. Serve with steamed broccoli and my Horiatiki (Greek salad, page 224). Before serving, for those who are sensitive to it, it's perhaps best to debone and remove the tail and head, then prepare the fillets with a drizzle of olive oil and lemon juice and a sprinkle of sea salt and freshly ground black pepper.

1. Preheat the oven to 425°F. Line a large roasting pan with aluminum foil.

2. In a large oven-safe or cast-iron skillet, heat 2 tablespoons of the olive oil over medium-high heat. One at a time, fry the whole

branzino quickly on each side to get the skins golden, 1 to 2 minutes per side, adding more oil if needed.

3. Stuff the cavity of each fish with a sprig each of thyme and rosemary and sprinkle the oregano on the inside and outside. Drizzle the inside of each fish and coat the outsides with 2 tablespoons olive oil.

4. Layer the fennel rounds and parsley stems on the bottom of the prepared roasting pan, then put the branzino on top. Squeeze the juice of one lemon half over the fish and season liberally with salt and pepper. Drizzle with another 2 tablespoons olive oil and bake until the fish is just cooked through, 10 to 12 minutes.

5. Thinly slice the remaining lemon half.

6. When the fish are done, remove the heads, if you like, and debone the fish. Drizzle with the remaining olive oil and serve with the lemon slices, parsley, and fennel. Season with salt and pepper and serve.

SALMON with Sesame-Soy-Ginger Glaze & Coconut Rice

SERVES 4

¼ cup low-sodium soy sauce

¼ cup mirin (sweet rice wine)

2 tablespoons grated fresh ginger

1 tablespoon dark brown sugar

2 garlic cloves, minced

3 green onions, thinly chopped

4 salmon fillets (about 2 pounds)

2 tablespoons sesame seeds

Coconut Rice (page 222)

Fresh cilantro, for garnish

THIS SALMON IS SO SIMPLE TO MAKE, and it's one of my standbys for when I need dinner in under 30 minutes. I like to make extra glaze, as it will keep for up to a week and you can use it on other meats or even on Asian noodles.

1. Preheat the oven to 350°F. Line a heavy baking sheet or roasting pan with parchment paper.

2. In a saucepan, combine the soy sauce, mirin, ginger, brown sugar, and garlic. Bring the mixture to a boil over medium heat, then reduce the heat to low and stir in the green onions. Take the pan off the heat. Total cooking time will be about 5 minutes.

3. Put the fillets, skin-side down, on the prepared roasting pan. Drizzle half the glaze. Bake until almost cooked through, about 10 minutes. Drizzle the remaining glaze over the salmon fillets and sprinkle the tops with the sesame seeds. Return to the oven and bake until the salmon is done to your liking, 2 to 5 minutes more for medium.

4. Sprinkle with the cilantro to garnish. Serve with the Coconut Rice.

SOLE with Lemon, Tomato & Caper Sauce

¼ cup all-purpose flour

2 tablespoons extra-virgin olive oil

4 (3- to 4-ounce) fillets sole

Sea salt and freshly ground black pepper

¼ cup dry white wine

3 tablespoons fresh lemon juice

2 medium plum tomatoes, chopped

3 tablespoons unsalted butter

2 tablespoons drained capers

1 garlic clove, minced

3 tablespoons chopped fresh parsley

THE INSPIRATION FOR THIS RECIPE comes from a classic sole meunière that features lemon-butter sauce, but I like to add white wine and tomatoes as well.

Paired with a crisp glass of white wine or rosé, this is as close to classic perfection in a meal as you can get, and it takes less than 30 minutes. Serve it with lightly steamed haricots verts (crispy, thin green beans) or peppery broccoli rabe, and perhaps some wild rice.

1. Preheat the oven to 200°F. Line an oven-safe platter with paper towels and put the flour on a plate for dredging.

2. In a large skillet, heat the olive oil over medium heat. Lightly dredge the fish in the flour, shaking off the excess, then immediately put the fish in the pan, working in two batches if needed. Fry the fish lightly until just opaque, 3 to 4 minutes per side.

3. Transfer the fish to the paper towel–lined platter and keep them warm in the oven.

4. Deglaze the pan with the wine and lemon juice. Stir in the tomatoes, butter, capers, and garlic. Bring to a simmer to thicken a bit, about 4 minutes. Stir in the parsley.

5. Remove the sole fillets from the oven and plate topped with the sauce. Serve right away.

BEER-&-BUTTERMILK-BATTERED FRIED COD with New Potato Chips

SERVES 6

1 cup Bisquick baking mix

½ cup cornstarch

1 tablespoon Old Bay seasoning

1 teaspoon garlic powder

½ teaspoon salt

Pinch of freshly ground black pepper

1 (12-ounce) bottle pale ale

1 large egg, beaten

2 cups buttermilk

½ cup all-purpose flour

Canola oil, for frying (about ½ cup)

6 cod fillets (can be cut into chunky pieces)

1 lemon, sliced into wedges

New Potato Chips (recipe follows)

THIS "FISH FRY" IS INSPIRED BY MY NEW LIFE IN CALIFORNIA, and it's also a great way to get my kids to eat fish! This is the champion of all summer comfort foods, but better than the beach boardwalk or seaside restaurant. Yeah, so it's battered and fried, but it doesn't really have that deep-fried flavor or feel. Maybe it's the buttermilk and beer that whip it up to a certain lightness . . . whatever it is, I can't resist it. Serve with corn on the cob and crisp new potato chips.

1. In a large bowl, combine the Bisquick, cornstarch, Old Bay, garlic powder, salt, and pepper. Whisk in the beer and egg to form a fluffy batter. Let the batter sit for about 15 minutes to allow the beer to settle. (In the meantime, start working on your New Potato Chips!)

2. Pour the buttermilk into a shallow bowl, and spread the flour out on a plate for dredging. Line a baking sheet with paper towels and set a wire rack over the pan.

3. In a large deep skillet, heat the canola oil over medium-high heat until it shimmers slightly. (If you have a deep fryer, you can of course use it instead.)

4. Pat the fish dry with paper towels. Season with salt and pepper.

5. Working with one at a time, coat the fillets with buttermilk, letting the excess drip off. Next, dredge each fillet in the flour, then dip them straight into the beer batter, liberally coating the fillets.

recipe continues

6. Fry a few pieces at a time for 3 minutes on each side until golden.

7. Drain the beer-battered cod on the prepared wire rack. Squeeze a lemon wedge over the top and serve right away with the New Potato Chips.

NEW POTATO CHIPS

SERVES 4 TO 6

2 cups very thinly sliced (⅛-inch-thick) new potatoes

3 tablespoons extra-virgin olive oil

1 teaspoon sweet paprika

½ teaspoon coarse sea salt

Pinch of freshly ground black pepper

¼ cup chopped fresh parsley

1. Preheat the oven to 450°F. Line a baking sheet with parchment paper.

2. Put the potatoes in a bowl, drizzle with the olive oil, then coat with the paprika, salt, pepper, and, finally, the parsley.

3. Lay the chips out on the baking sheet so that they are spread out in a single layer, not touching. Bake for 15 minutes on one side, then, using a spatula, flip the chips to the other side and bake until both sides are crispy and golden, 8 to 10 minutes. Keep an eye on these as cooking times can vary (and burn quickly!). Serve with the crispy fried cod.

VEGETARIAN

BLACK BEAN VEGGIE BURGER

VEGETARIAN
SERVES 6

1 sweet potato

½ cup diced mushrooms

¼ cup minced yellow onion

1 garlic clove, minced

1 (15-ounce) can black beans, drained and rinsed

1 cup whole wheat bread crumbs

½ cup cooked quinoa (prepared according to the package instructions)

1 large egg, beaten

1 tablespoon Worcestershire sauce

1 teaspoon chili powder

1 teaspoon salt

¼ teaspoon freshly ground black pepper

Nonstick cooking spray

Toppings of your choice

WHILE I DO LOVE MY BURGERS made with beef or turkey, on occasion I crave a leaner, healthier option, and these black bean veggie burgers do the trick. I also make them as a vegetarian option when we're having a barbecue, to make sure there is something for everyone. By adding the right combination of spices and flavors, you can truly simulate the taste and even the texture of a juicy beef burger. These veggie burgers also hold up well on a grill; just make sure you spray plenty of nonstick spray on the grill first. You can also bake them in the oven, if you prefer.

1. Line a large bowl with paper towels and line a baking sheet with parchment paper.

2. Microwave the sweet potato until it is soft, 5 to 6 minutes, then cut it in half and scoop out the flesh.

3. In a food processor, pulse the mushrooms, onion, and garlic together. Scoop the mixture into the bowl lined with paper towels and squeeze out any extra moisture.

4. Quickly pulse the black beans in the food processor until coarsely chopped but not mushy.

5. Remove and discard the paper towel from the bowl with the mushroom mixture, then add the sweet potato, black beans, bread crumbs, quinoa, egg, Worcestershire, chili powder, salt, and

recipe continues

pepper. Mix with your hands. Form the mixture into 1-inch-thick patties and arrange them on the prepared baking sheet. Refrigerate the patties for at least 30 minutes or up to overnight to firm them up.

6. Heat a grill to 400 to 450°F or preheat the oven to 450°F. If grilling, spray the grill racks liberally with a nonstick spray.

7. Grill the black bean burgers until a crust forms on the outside and the burgers are warmed through, 4 to 5 minutes on each side. (If you are baking the burgers, leave them on the baking sheet and bake for 8 to 10 minutes on each side.)

8. Serve as a regular burger, with all the toppings you like.

RED & WHITE BEANS with Red Peppers, Green Beans & Quinoa

GLUTEN-FREE
VEGETARIAN
SERVES 8

2 cups quinoa

3 tablespoons extra-virgin olive oil

½ white onion, diced (about 1 cup)

2 garlic cloves, minced

1 pound fresh green beans, cut into
1-inch pieces

1 red bell pepper, chopped

1 (15-ounce) can cannellini beans,
drained and rinsed

1 (15-ounce) can red kidney beans,
drained and rinsed

1 teaspoon fresh thyme leaves,
or ½ teaspoon dried

1 teaspoon minced fresh oregano,
or ½ teaspoon dried

½ cup chopped fresh parsley

1 tablespoon balsamic vinegar

Salt and freshly ground black pepper

Splash of Tabasco or other hot sauce,
for serving (optional)

KEEP IT SIMPLE by using canned white cannellini beans and red kidney beans (if you prefer to use dried beans, just soak them overnight and prepare as instructed). This bean and veggie dish can be made well in advance and served at any temperature, for added convenience. Make it on the weekends for a full week of great meals; it works equally well as a side dish or a lunchtime salad. For the non-vegetarians in your home, you can add tuna, cooked low-fat turkey sausage, or grilled chicken.

1. Prepare the quinoa as instructed on the package and set aside.

2. In a very large skillet, heat 1 tablespoon of the olive oil over medium heat. Add the onion and garlic and cook, stirring, until the onion is slightly softened, about 2 minutes.

3. Add the green beans and bell pepper and cook until they are a bit tender, though they will still be al dente, about 4 minutes.

4. Stir in the cannellini and red kidney beans and cook until the green beans and peppers are to your liking, 6 to 8 minutes. Sprinkle in the thyme and oregano.

5. In a large bowl, stir together the quinoa, beans, and vegetables. Add the parsley and drizzle with the remaining 2 tablespoons olive oil and the vinegar. Toss to mix. Season with salt and black pepper and serve with Tabasco, if desired, for a kick.

CURRIED QUINOA with Sweet Potato & Chickpeas

GLUTEN-FREE
VEGETARIAN
SERVES 8

2 tablespoons extra-virgin olive oil

1 cup diced yellow onion

1 tablespoon minced fresh ginger

1 garlic clove, minced

1 tablespoon curry paste

1 tablespoon garam masala

2 cups diced sweet potatoes
(¼-inch cubes; from about
1 large sweet potato)

1 (14-ounce) can chickpeas,
drained and rinsed

1 cup canned diced tomatoes
with juices

2 cups vegetable broth

½ teaspoon ground nutmeg

1 cup quinoa

Salt and freshly ground black pepper

1 cup chopped baby spinach

¼ cup chopped fresh cilantro

2 tablespoons fresh lime juice

TRY ANOTHER DELICIOUS QUINOA RECIPE, with a Middle Eastern twist this time. There's an addictive blend of sweetness and spice, and it's filled with goodness. You can also make this in advance and serve it at your preferred temperature. I like to pack it for lunch, too, as it's a meal-in-one that keeps me full and energized throughout the day.

1. In a large Dutch oven, heat the olive oil over medium heat. Add the onion, ginger, garlic, curry paste, and garam masala. Cook, stirring continuously, until the onion is soft, 3 to 5 minutes.

2. Stir in the sweet potatoes, chickpeas, tomatoes with their juices, 1 cup of the broth, and the nutmeg. Increase the heat to medium-high and when it starts to boil, add the quinoa. Stir in the remaining 1 cup broth and reduce the heat to medium-low. Cover the pot and simmer until the liquid has been absorbed and the quinoa is cooked, 20 to 25 minutes.

3. Remove the curry from the heat, fluff with a fork, and let cool for 5 to 10 minutes. Season with salt and pepper, then stir in the chopped spinach, cilantro, and lime juice as you serve.

WARM BRUSSELS SPROUT SALAD with Butternut & Cremini

VEGETARIAN
SERVES 4 TO 6

THIS RECIPE IS INSPIRED BY THE YEARS I LIVED IN SPAIN, where Brussels sprouts get much more respect. Served as a hearty warm entrée salad or as a side, it's a great dish to pull out when entertaining vegetarian friends.

VINAIGRETTE

½ cup sherry vinegar

¼ cup extra-virgin olive oil

2 tablespoons minced shallot (about 1 large shallot)

1 tablespoon Dijon mustard

1 teaspoon honey

½ teaspoon salt

SALAD

¾ cup vegetable broth

3 tablespoons extra-virgin olive oil

1 pound Brussels sprouts, halved

1 cup diced butternut squash (½-inch cubes)

Salt and freshly ground black pepper

1 cup halved cremini mushrooms

½ red onion, very thinly sliced

1 garlic clove, minced

1 cup canned chickpeas, drained and rinsed

2 tablespoons fresh thyme leaves

1. **Make the vinaigrette:** In a bowl, whisk together the vinegar, olive oil, shallot, mustard, honey, and salt. Set aside.

2. **Make the salad:** In a large sauté pan, heat the broth and 2 tablespoons of the olive oil over medium heat. When simmering, put the Brussels sprouts cut-side down in the pan and add the butternut squash. Season with salt and pepper and allow the sprouts and squash to cook until tender, about 10 minutes. When the broth has evaporated, allow the vegetables to caramelize to a golden brown, 10 to 15 minutes more. Remove from the pan and set aside.

3. In the same pan, heat the remaining 1 tablespoon olive oil over medium heat. Add the mushrooms, onion, and garlic and cook, stirring frequently, until tender, about 4 minutes.

4. Add the vinaigrette to the pan. Stir in the chickpeas and thyme and cook for 2 minutes. Return the Brussels sprouts and butternut squash to the pan and stir to warm, about 1 minute. Season with salt and pepper and serve.

Variation: If you want a bit more flavor and don't care if it's vegetarian, fry up ¼ cup diced pancetta or Serrano ham until crispy and stir in right before serving.

PASTA PRIMAVERA

VEGETARIAN
SERVES 4

1 (16-ounce) box pasta, such as farfalle
(bow ties) or rigatoni

¼ cup extra-virgin olive oil

2 cups chopped broccoli florets

6 asparagus spears, cut into ½-inch pieces

2 green onions, thinly sliced

2 garlic cloves, minced

1 cup quartered cherry tomatoes

Salt and freshly ground black pepper

1 cup frozen peas

½ teaspoon grated lemon zest

2 tablespoons fresh lemon juice

1 tablespoon finely chopped fresh oregano

1 tablespoon finely chopped
fresh parsley or basil

1 teaspoon minced fresh thyme leaves

⅓ cup freshly grated Parmesan cheese

THE WONDERFUL THING ABOUT PASTA PRIMAVERA is that it is so delicious and fresh, and a great vehicle, once again, for any vegetables you have that you need to use. You can do an all-green primavera with peas, broccoli, and asparagus, or add fresh cherry tomatoes, chopped parsley or basil, and plenty of herbs, a dash of garlic, and some lemon zest and juice to add flavor to the pasta.

The key to this pasta? Don't throw out all the cooking water after boiling the pasta. That starchy water works as a thickener for your sauce. My husband loves this dish even more when I fry up ½ pound of chopped prosciutto and crush it up for a little extra flavor. It's no longer vegetarian at that point but it's a delicious option if you want to take it to that level.

1. Bring a large pot of salted water to a boil. Cook the pasta according to the package instructions until al dente.

2. Meanwhile, in a separate skillet, heat the olive oil over medium-high heat. Add the broccoli, asparagus, green onions, and garlic and cook, stirring, until the broccoli and asparagus are firm but tender, making sure they do not brown, about 2 minutes. Add the tomatoes to the skillet and cook, stirring, for 2 minutes more. Season with salt and pepper.

3. Reserve 1 cup of the pasta cooking water, then drain the pasta and return it to the pasta pot over medium heat. Stir in the sautéed vegetables. Toss with the reserved 1 cup pasta water, the

Note: For an easy variation, add homemade pesto to give it even more pizzazz. And I love adding good-for-you legumes to give the pasta a protein boost. Fava, cannellini beans, or garbanzo beans are all great options. Just add them in with the vegetables in the last three minutes of cooking, so they don't overcook but will still soak up the flavors. For the pescetarian, I recommend adding poached salmon (see recipe on page 57). Canned tuna is great too, or if you prefer a fresh, white flaky fish, just cook it separately, cut it into bite-size pieces, and mix it in with the pasta. For the meat eater, this is a good vehicle for chopped leftover rotisserie chicken or beef.

peas, lemon zest, lemon juice, oregano, parsley, and thyme. Cook until the water has mostly been absorbed.

4. Sprinkle with the Parmesan and toss. Season with salt and pepper and serve immediately.

If you have leftovers, just add fresh mozzarella chunks, chopped olives (optional), some chopped basil and oregano, and salad dressing and you have a delicious ready-to-eat pasta salad. Or, pasta frittata, anyone? You can have pasta for breakfast, lunch, or dinner with this option. Just beat 4 eggs with 2 tablespoons of milk, a pinch of salt and pepper, and stir in about 1 cup of the leftover pasta. Mix well, then coat a medium skillet with olive oil and cook the frittata over medium heat. When the eggs firm up and the bottom becomes golden, carefully place a plate on top of the skillet and flip the frittata onto the plate, then slide it back into the skillet to cook the other side.

HEALTHIER MAC & CHEESE

VEGETARIAN
SERVES 4 TO 6

½ teaspoon salt,
plus more for the pasta water

1 (16-ounce) box elbow macaroni (whole
wheat or gluten-free, if you prefer)

1 tablespoon unsalted butter

2½ cups chopped cauliflower

1½ cups cubed peeled butternut squash

2 green onions, thinly sliced

4 cups vegetable broth

¾ cup low-fat evaporated milk
(unsweetened condensed milk)

Pinch of freshly ground black pepper

Nonstick cooking spray or olive oil spray

½ cup grated Gruyère cheese

¼ cup shredded part skim
mozzarella cheese

¼ cup freshly grated Parmesan cheese

1 teaspoon chopped fresh thyme leaves

1 teaspoon smoked paprika

3 tablespoons whole wheat
Italian bread crumbs

NOTHING SAYS COMFORT FOOD LIKE MAC AND CHEESE, and there is probably nothing I crave more some days. While it's okay to indulge (once in a blue moon) in the real deal, I do think if you can find ways to make your favorites a little lighter and healthier, then why not try? One nip and tuck: Add vegetables like cauliflower and butternut squash to cream it up but also to fortify it with all their nutrients (plus, the butternut squash gives it that little bit of orange color like that no-good-for-you stuff out of the box). But this does not mean we are getting rid of the cheese altogether, oh no. It wouldn't be mac and cheese without cheese, after all. But we will be going a bit lighter there, too—the key is mixing it up . . . Follow along and enjoy.

1. Bring a large pot of salted water to a boil. Cook the pasta according to the package instructions. Drain and set aside.

2. In the empty pasta pot, melt the butter over medium heat. Add the cauliflower, squash, and green onion. Cook, stirring continuously, until the vegetables are slightly tender but not browned, about 4 minutes. Add the broth and cook until more tender, 8 minutes more. Drain the vegetables, reserving the cooking liquid.

3. In a blender, combine the evaporated milk, 1 cup of the vegetable cooking liquid, the vegetables, salt, and pepper. Let cool, if necessary, then blend in batches, if needed, until it becomes a

recipe continues

creamy puree (be careful when blending hot liquids). Blend in the remaining 3 cups vegetable cooking liquid.

4. Preheat the oven to broil. Spray a deep baking dish or lasagna dish with nonstick spray or olive oil spray.

5. In the same pasta pot, mix the cooked pasta with the Gruyère, mozzarella, and Parmesan cheeses and the vegetable puree. Season with the thyme and paprika and salt to taste. Cook over medium heat, stirring, until the cheese has melted evenly.

6. Spread the pasta mixture in the prepared dish and sprinkle the whole wheat bread crumbs on top. Pop in the oven and broil until the top and the cheese become a little golden and crisp, just 3 quick minutes, then serve right away!

CLASSIC MUSHROOM & PEA RISOTTO

GLUTEN-FREE
VEGETARIAN
SERVES 6 TO 8

2 tablespoons extra-virgin olive oil

½ yellow onion, finely chopped

2 cups Arborio rice

2 tablespoons unsalted butter

¾ cup dry white wine

1 teaspoon grated lemon zest

4 cups vegetable broth, warmed

2 cups warm water

1 cup chopped cremini
or white button mushrooms

1 cup thawed frozen or shelled fresh peas

¼ cup freshly grated Parmesan cheese

Salt and freshly ground black pepper

A RICH CLASSIC THAT IS HARD NOT TO LOVE, this risotto actually got my oldest son, Josh, to finally like mushrooms. Serve as a side dish or on its own, and you will be plenty satisfied. I love just the mushrooms and peas, but I have also used asparagus and have added prosciutto to change it up some. It all starts with a high-end short-grain Arborio rice and then just a bit of TLC to get it to the right creaminess. The key is to add the broth slowly over time while stirring pretty constantly. You want it still al dente, but creamy—not heavy and sticky.

1. In a 6- to 8-quart pot, heat the olive oil over medium heat. Add the onion and cook, stirring, until transparent, about 4 minutes—don't let the onion brown. Stir in the rice and coat the grains with the oil. Add the butter and cook for about a minute.

2. Add the wine and lemon zest and stir until the wine has been absorbed. Cook, stirring periodically as you add the warm broth and water in ½-cup portions so that it covers the rice. Ten minutes in, add the mushrooms. After 15 minutes, add the peas (you want them to stay a vibrant green). The total cooking time is 20 to 25 minutes. Continue adding the water and broth, stirring continuously, until you reach the right texture, which should be slightly al dente.

3. When done, serve it in a big bowl. Stir in the Parmesan and season with salt and pepper.

KID FAVORITES

GRILLED CALIFORNIA BARBECUE CHICKEN PIZZA

SERVES 4

1 recipe Good Grilling Pizza Dough
(recipe follows)

1½ cups chopped cooked chicken
(use leftover rotisserie chicken or
chicken breast)

1 cup store-bought barbecue sauce
(I love Bone Suckin' Sauce, mild)

Semolina flour, for dusting

6 tablespoons extra-virgin olive oil

½ cup thinly sliced red onions

½ cup thinly sliced mushrooms

2 cups shredded mozzarella cheese

½ cup shredded smoked Gouda cheese

Salt and freshly ground black pepper

2 tablespoons chopped fresh cilantro,
for garnish

I OFTEN TAKE INSPIRATION from some of my kids' favorite restaurants, like I did for this California Barbecue Chicken Pizza, which is a little bit like the California Pizza Kitchen's, and you can make it on the grill. I love grilling pizza because it actually works better for pizza than your oven, as it tends to get much hotter, which makes for a crispier crust. The key to grilling pizza with success is to grill the dough a little bit first, prior to piling on your toppings.

1. Prepare or defrost the pizza dough.

2. Heat a grill to its highest setting. You want to cover it as well while heating so that the heat stays trapped. Ideally you are trying to get it to 500 to 550°F.

3. In a bowl, coat the chicken pieces with 2 to 3 tablespoons of the barbecue sauce, saving the rest for the pizza crust.

4. Brush two half sheet pans with 2 tablespoons of the olive oil each. Sprinkle some semolina onto a clean counter and roll out the dough balls, one at a time, into rectangles about 10 by 15 inches each. The crust should be a little thicker than the usual thin crust to make sure it stays intact on the grill. Move the rolled dough onto the prepared sheet pans and brush the top of each with the remaining olive oil. Now you're ready to grill the pizzas.

5. For each pizza, slide the dough into the grill and cook, uncovered, until the dough begins to bubble, about 2 minutes, then flip it over using a large spatula and cook for an additional minute.

recipe continues

6. Transfer the pizza crusts onto two large platters and quickly add the toppings: Layer on the barbecue sauce first, leaving a ½-inch border around the edge of the dough. Then top evenly with the red onions, mushrooms, and chicken. Top with the mozzarella, followed by the Gouda. Be careful not to overload your pizzas, as you don't want them to be too heavy and fall apart.

7. Slide the pizzas back onto the grill and cover it. Allow the pizzas to cook until the cheese melts and the crusts are crispy, about 5 minutes.

8. Remove the pizzas, then sprinkle them with the cilantro to garnish. Cut into slices and enjoy the best barbecue chicken grilled pizza you will ever have.

GOOD GRILLING PIZZA DOUGH

MAKES ENOUGH FOR
TWO 12-INCH PIZZAS

1½ cups lukewarm water

2 teaspoons active dry yeast

3 tablespoons extra-virgin olive oil, plus
more for coating the dough

5 cups Italian "00" flour (or superlight
and fine flour, such as White Lily Light
AP baking flour)

1 teaspoon salt

1. Put the lukewarm water in a large bowl, then whisk in the yeast and let it sit until the water froths a bit, about 8 minutes.

2. Stir the olive oil into the water mixture. Add the flour and salt, and knead the dough by hand for about 6 minutes (or transfer to the bowl of a stand mixer fitted with the dough hook and knead that way). The dough should be springy and stretchy.

3. Cut the dough into 2 balls, then coat with olive oil. Place the balls next to each other on a baking sheet, covered with a clean, damp dishtowel. Let the dough rise for a few hours until it's about double in size.

4. Use the dough right away or refrigerate/freeze if you are using it later. If refrigerated, use the dough within 1 day, but it can remain frozen for up to 1 week. Simply thaw for about 3 hours at room temperature or until the dough is once again soft and pliable.

TACO TUESDAY CHICKEN TACOS

SERVES 4 TO 6

1½ pounds chicken breast

½ teaspoon salt

¼ teaspoon freshly ground black pepper

2 tablespoons extra-virgin olive oil

¼ cup chopped white onion

1 (14.5-ounce) can diced tomatoes with juices

⅓ cup fresh lime juice

2 garlic cloves, minced

1 tablespoon chili powder

2 teaspoons red wine vinegar

1 teaspoon ground cumin

1 teaspoon dried oregano

½ teaspoon sugar

8 to 12 tortilla shells of your choosing (we like 6-inch corn tortillas)

Note: If you're using rotisserie chicken or precooked chicken, prepare the taco sauce as directed, then add the shredded cooked chicken and let it simmer for 10 to 15 in the sauce minutes to really soak in the sauce.

HAVING THEME NIGHTS, like Meat Loaf Mondays, Taco Tuesdays, or Breakfast-for-Dinner Saturdays makes dinner more of an "event," something the kids can plan on and look forward to. These tacos are a weeknight must for days they have to get out the door fast for sports/games in the evening. I often use leftover grilled chicken or rotisserie chicken to speed things up even more, but if you are starting from scratch, it's still super quick and simple. Make a platter with toppings, such as sour cream, Mexican crema, chopped tomatoes, finely chopped lettuce or cabbage, onions, cilantro, and fresh lime wedges to garnish, and let your kids build their own, as they are more likely to try new things this way.

---

1. Season the chicken breasts with the salt and pepper.

2. In a large skillet, heat the olive oil over medium heat. Cook the chicken until golden, about 3 minutes per side. Add the onion and cook, stirring, until slightly translucent, about 2 minutes. Stir in the tomatoes with their juices, lime juice, garlic, chili powder, vinegar, cumin, oregano, and sugar. Reduce the heat and simmer, uncovered, stirring frequently, until the chicken is cooked through, about 15 minutes.

3. Transfer the chicken to a cutting board. Use two forks to shred the meat, then transfer it back to the skillet. To allow the taco sauce to really seep into the shredded chicken, simmer for 5 to 8 minutes more.

4. If you're using soft shells, warm the tortillas, sandwiched between damp paper towels, for about 30 seconds in the microwave. If you're using hard shells, put them in a 250°F oven until warm, about 5 minutes. Serve.

FISH TACOS

2 cups panko bread crumbs

2 large eggs, beaten

1 cup all-purpose flour

1 tablespoon chili powder

1 tablespoon salt

1 teaspoon garlic powder

1 teaspoon onion powder

1 teaspoon ground cumin

½ teaspoon freshly ground black pepper

1 pound haddock or white cod,
cut into 1-inch-long strips

1 cup vegetable oil or canola oil, for frying

8 (6-inch) corn tortillas

To garnish: Finely shredded cabbage,
chopped tomatoes, cilantro, lime wedges,
and Sriracha Aioli (recipe follows)

SOUTHERN CALIFORNIA HAS THE BEST FISH TACOS you will ever try, and I do try them a lot. There are so many ways to make them, but I like a lightly battered fish, as it absorbs some of the other flavors better. Try using a haddock or flaky white cod, as they hold up best, and top with Sriracha Aioli. Here is my how-to on the crispy fish.

---

1. Put the panko in a shallow bowl; put the eggs in a separate shallow bowl.

2. In a large bowl, whisk together the flour, chili powder, salt, garlic powder, onion powder, cumin, and pepper. Add the fish strips to the bowl, coating all the pieces evenly.

3. Line a large plate with paper towels. In a large skillet, heat the vegetable oil over medium-high heat. When a small pinch of panko dropped into the oil sizzles and floats to the top, it's ready for frying.

4. Dredge the fish into the beaten eggs first, then coat on all sides with the panko.

5. Working in batches, fry the fish pieces, turning as needed, until all sides are golden, about 7 minutes total. Remove the fish and drain on the paper towel–lined plate.

6. Warm the tortillas, sandwiched between damp paper towels, for about 30 seconds in the microwave. Put a couple of strips of fish in each tortilla and top with shredded cabbage, tomatoes, cilantro, a squeeze of fresh lime, and a drizzle of Sriracha Aioli.

SRIRACHA AIOLI

½ cup mayonnaise

2 tablespoons Sriracha

1 tablespoon fresh lemon juice

In a small bowl, stir together the mayonnaise, Sriracha, and lemon juice. Serve immediately or refrigerate until needed.

HEALTHIER CHICKEN NUGGETS

SERVES 4 TO 6

2 pounds chicken breasts (about 4)

Kosher salt

2 large eggs

1 cup seasoned whole wheat bread crumbs

¼ cup semolina flour

¼ cup freshly grated Parmesan cheese

1 tablespoon chopped fresh parsley

1 teaspoon onion powder

1 teaspoon dried thyme

1 teaspoon dried oregano

¼ teaspoon freshly ground black pepper

1 tablespoon extra-virgin olive oil

MY KIDS HAVE EATEN JUST ABOUT EVERY KIND OF CHICKEN NUGGET. Sadly, it is a food group all on its own to them. But many frozen or store-bought nuggets are made with fillers and other not-so-good-for-you ingredients. The solution? Make them yourself. Once you do, you'll see how simple and delicious they are. Bake large quantities so you can freeze them for future use.

1. Preheat the oven to 425°F. Line a baking sheet with parchment paper.

2. Cut the chicken breasts into 2-inch morsels and sprinkle with a bit of salt.

3. Beat the eggs in a bowl to make an egg wash.

4. In a large plastic bag, combine the bread crumbs, semolina, Parmesan, parsley, onion powder, thyme, oregano, 1 teaspoon salt, and the pepper.

5. Dredge the chicken pieces first in the egg, then toss them into the plastic bag and give the bag a good shake to coat them completely.

6. Arrange the chicken on the lined baking sheet. Drizzle them with the olive oil. Bake for about 8 minutes, then flip and bake for 8 minutes more, until both sides are golden and the chicken is cooked. Serve immediately.

SPAGHETTI & MINI-MEATBALL BAKE

SERVES 6 TO 8

1 pound lean ground beef (93% lean is preferable) or ground turkey, if you really want to go lean

½ cup seasoned whole wheat bread crumbs

½ cup whole or 2% milk

½ cup freshly grated Parmesan cheese

2 large eggs

1 tablespoon minced garlic

1 tablespoon chopped fresh parsley

1 (16-ounce) container low-fat ricotta cheese

12 ounces uncooked spaghetti or whole wheat spaghetti noodles broken in half

1 (32-ounce) jar marinara sauce

1 tablespoon chopped fresh basil

½ pound fresh mozzarella, sliced

NOTHING SAYS HOME-COOKED COMFORT FOOD better than baked spaghetti and meatballs. Kids love this mini-meatball bake because you get a perfect bite-size meatball with the right amount of sauce and noodles. But the most fantastic part about this recipe is that it's all done in one large baking dish—no frying the meatballs or cooking the noodles ahead of time. It's amazing and *so* delicious! Serve with garlic bread and a side salad and you have the perfect dinner.

1. Preheat the oven to 400°F.

2. In a large bowl, combine the ground beef, bread crumbs, milk, ¼ cup of the Parmesan, the eggs, garlic, and parsley. Using your hands, mix all the ingredients well. Form the meat mixture into 1-inch meatballs (you should have about 30 meatballs). Set aside on a baking sheet.

3. Spread a layer of the ricotta over the bottom of a casserole dish. Then layer the broken spaghetti noodles on top of the ricotta.

4. In a large bowl, mix together the marinara sauce, ½ cup water, and the basil. Pour onto the noodles, making sure they are well covered.

5. Top with the uncooked meatballs, spreading them evenly.

6. Cover the dish with aluminum foil and bake for 45 to 50 minutes, stirring once, to ensure the meatballs and noodles get cooked.

7. Sprinkle the top with the remaining Parmesan cheese, then cover with the mozzarella. Set the oven to broil and broil the casserole, uncovered, until the cheese has melted and the top is golden, about 5 minutes.

HAPPY FAMILY CHICKEN-&-SHRIMP STIR-FRY

SERVES 4

¾ cup beef broth

3 tablespoons low-sodium soy sauce

3 tablespoons dry cooking wine or sherry

2 tablespoons dark brown sugar

2 tablespoons oyster sauce

1 tablespoon plus 2 teaspoons toasted sesame oil

1 tablespoon canola oil

3 garlic cloves, minced

1 tablespoon minced ginger

2 cups thinly sliced chicken breast strips (about ½ inch thick)

1½ cups peeled and deveined jumbo shrimp

¾ cup chopped broccoli florets

½ cup thinly sliced carrots (sliced into coins)

½ cup canned baby corn, drained

½ cup straw mushrooms or thinly sliced shiitakes

½ cup snow peas

½ cup chopped red bell pepper

¼ cup canned water chestnuts, drained

¼ cup canned sliced bamboo shoots, drained

1 tablespoon cornstarch, mixed with 1 tablespoon water to make a slurry

½ cup thinly sliced green onions

Salt

Pinch of red pepper flakes

GROWING UP, ONE OF MY FAVORITE Chinese takeout orders was the Happy Family, a stir-fry with chicken, pork, beef, and shrimp that's loaded with veggies and served with rice or rice noodles. It lives up to its name, as there's a mix of everything for everyone—but making this recipe a bit healthier and leaner makes me especially happy for my family. You can add lean pork slices or beef if you prefer it the more traditional way. There are no rules; the only requirement is to love it.

1. In a medium bowl, stir together the broth, soy sauce, cooking wine, brown sugar, oyster sauce, and 2 teaspoons of the sesame oil. Set aside.

2. In large skillet or wok, heat the remaining 1 tablespoon sesame oil and the canola oil over medium-high heat. Add the garlic and ginger and cook, stirring, until fragrant, just a few seconds. Stir in the chicken and cook, stirring, until opaque and starting to brown, 1 to 2 minutes, then add the shrimp. Cook, stirring, until the shrimp are no longer translucent, about 2 minutes. Remove the chicken and shrimp and reserve for later.

3. Stir in the broccoli, carrots, baby corn, mushrooms, snow peas, bell pepper, water chestnuts, and bamboo shoots and cook, stirring, until the vegetables are crisp-tender, 3 to 4 minutes.

4. Stir in the sauce and the cornstarch slurry until incorporated. Add the chicken and shrimp and the green onions to the wok. Cook, stirring, until the sauce has coated the ingredients well and thickened a bit, about 3 minutes. Taste for seasoning and adjust as needed with salt and red pepper flakes. Serve immediately.

SNEAKY TURKEY QUINOA LASAGNA

SERVES 8

2 tablespoons extra-virgin olive oil

½ cup minced white onion

2 garlic cloves, minced

2 cups packed fresh baby spinach, finely chopped

1 cup chopped white mushrooms

1 pound 93% lean ground turkey

1 cup cooked quinoa (prepared according to the package instructions)

Salt and freshly ground black pepper

1 (25-ounce) jar prepared marinara sauce

½ cup red wine

2 tablespoons chopped fresh basil

1 tablespoon fresh chopped oregano, or 1 teaspoon dried

1 (30-ounce) tub low-fat ricotta cheese

½ cup freshly grated Parmesan cheese

2 large eggs

¼ cup chopped fresh parsley

I CALL THIS MY SNEAKY TURKEY LASAGNA because I pack it with so much nutrition—finely chopped mushrooms, spinach, and the tomato sauce give you all the vegetables you need in one serving. And once again, quinoa, the perfect food, is a great source of added protein while also giving the ground turkey a nice crunch. You can also use quinoa in a vegetarian version, with sautéed vegetables instead of turkey meat.

I make lasagnas on the weekends to have during the week. Just pop it in the oven when you're ready for dinner. This is also a wonderful meal for entertaining, as it's a crowd-pleaser, feeds many people, and allows you to be social while it's baking away.

1. In a large Dutch oven or pot, heat the olive oil over medium heat. Stir in the onion and garlic and cook, stirring, until the onion begins to look translucent, 1 to 2 minutes. Stir in the spinach and mushrooms and cook, stirring, until the mushrooms are just tender, 3 to 4 minutes. Remove the vegetables and set aside.

2. Add the ground turkey to the pot and cook, using a wooden spoon to break it up, until no longer pink, 8 to 10 minutes. Stir in the quinoa and mix it evenly with the turkey meat. Season with salt and pepper.

3. Return the spinach and mushrooms to the pot and stir into the meat. Add the marinara sauce, wine, basil, and oregano and simmer over medium-low heat until it reduces a little, about 20 minutes.

4. Meanwhile, in a large bowl, blend together the ricotta, Parmesan, eggs, and parsley and season with salt and pepper. Set aside.

5. Preheat the oven to 375°F.

6. **Make the béchamel sauce:** In a medium saucepan, melt the butter over medium heat, then mix in the flour with a wooden spoon. Slowly pour in the milk and whisk until the sauce starts to thicken and lightly boil, about 5 minutes. Season with the nutmeg and salt and pepper to taste. Remove from the heat when it becomes thick and creamy.

7. In a large lasagna dish or other baking dish, spread a layer of the turkey tomato sauce, then pour on a thin layer of the béchamel sauce. Add a layer of 4 no-boil noodles, then spread a cup of the ricotta mixture on top. Add another layer of 4 noodles and any remaining béchamel. Spoon the rest of the turkey tomato sauce on top and cover with the remaining 4 noodles. Spread the remaining ricotta mixture on top, sprinkle evenly with the shredded mozzarella, and then top with the sliced mozzarella.

8. Bake until the cheese melts and becomes golden, about 30 minutes. Enjoy for days!

BÉCHAMEL (WHITE) SAUCE

2 tablespoons unsalted butter

2 tablespoons all-purpose flour

1 cup 2% milk

Pinch of ground nutmeg

Salt and freshly ground black pepper

12 no-boil lasagna noodles

4 ounces shredded mozzarella cheese

5 or 6 slices fresh mozzarella cheese

TURKEY-QUINOA MEAT LOAF

GLUTEN-FREE
SERVES 4 TO 6

1 tablespoon extra-virgin olive oil

1 celery stalk, diced

¼ cup minced sweet onion

¼ cup finely shredded or minced carrots

¼ cup diced mushrooms

2 garlic cloves, minced

1½ pounds 93% lean ground turkey

1 cup cooked quinoa (prepared according to the package instructions)

¼ cup minced fresh parsley

1 large egg

2 tablespoons Worcestershire sauce

1 tablespoon tomato paste

1 teaspoon salt

½ teaspoon freshly ground black pepper

GLAZE

1 tablespoon ketchup

1 tablespoon dark brown sugar, dissolved with 1 teaspoon water

1 teaspoon Worcestershire sauce

WHO DOESN'T LOVE A GOOD MEAT LOAF? It's the ultimate comfort food, though a bit hearty and heavy made the ordinary way. Not this turkey-quinoa variation—it packs lean protein and vegetables all in a single serving. I sneak in mushrooms, celery, and shredded carrots for added nutrition that my kids hardly notice. Best part about this meat loaf is that it makes great sandwiches for lunch the next day and almost tastes better a day or two later.

Serve the meat loaf with a heaping plate of steamed vegetables or roasted potatoes (instead of mashed potatoes) for a healthier complete meal.

1. Preheat the oven to 350°F. Line an 8½ by 4½-inch loaf pan with parchment paper.

2. In a medium skillet, heat the olive oil over medium-high heat. Add the celery, onion, carrots, mushrooms, and garlic and cook, stirring, until the vegetables soften and the mushrooms have released their moisture, 5 to 7 minutes.

3. In a large bowl, mix the ground turkey, quinoa, parsley, egg, Worcestershire, tomato paste, cooked vegetables, salt, and pepper. It will be a very moist mixture. Shape the ground turkey mixture into the prepared loaf pan.

4. **Make the glaze:** In a small bowl, mix the ketchup, brown sugar mixture, and Worcestershire. Brush the glaze over the top of the meat loaf.

5. Bake the meat loaf for 45 to 50 minutes, until the turkey is cooked through and not pink. If hot liquid settles on the top by the end of cooking, carefully pour it off and dab it away with a paper towel before unmolding and serving.

BEEF-ONION BURGER

1½ pounds 93% lean ground beef

1 large egg

½ ounce onion soup mix
(½ of a 1-ounce packet)

1 tablespoon Worcestershire sauce

½ teaspoon salt

Pinch of freshly ground black pepper

6 slices Swiss cheese (optional)

6 hamburger buns (optional)

Caramelized Onions and Mushrooms
(recipe follows)

Sliced avocado (optional)

A DELICIOUS JUICY ONION BURGER JUST MAY BE THE WAY STRAIGHT TO MY HEART. Pile it high with caramelized mushrooms, onions, avocado, and melted Swiss. Yes, this is a total splurge meal, but if you do want to keep it reasonable, eliminate the buns and serve a salad or steamed vegetables on the side. You have here a high-protein meal that will at least keep your burger craving in check for a while.

1. Put the ground beef in a large bowl and let it come to room temperature, 15 to 20 minutes.

2. Heat a grill or grill pan to medium-high, about 400°F on a grill gauge.

3. Crack the egg into the meat and add the onion soup mix and Worcestershire. Mix thoroughly, seasoning with the salt and pepper. Shape into six 1-inch-thick burger patties.

4. Grill the patties with the grill closed, aside from flipping them, until cooked to your liking (160°F internal temperature is the USDA recommendation). To keep the meat juicy, don't press on the patties. We cook our burgers to medium, about 6 minutes on each side. Add cheese slices for the last 2 minutes of cooking, if desired.

5. Place patties on the buns, if using, and top with Caramelized Onions and Mushrooms and avocado slices, if desired.

CARAMELIZED ONIONS & MUSHROOMS

1 tablespoon extra-virgin olive oil

1 sweet onion, halved, then thinly sliced

1 teaspoon unsalted butter

Salt

1 cup thinly sliced mushrooms

1 tablespoon dry white wine

2 tablespoons chopped fresh parsley

Freshly ground black pepper

1. In a large skillet, heat the olive oil over medium heat. Add the onion and cook, stirring frequently, until translucent, 7 to 8 minutes.

2. Add the butter and cook, stirring frequently to keep them from sticking or burning, until golden, about 10 minutes. Sprinkle with a dash of salt and 1 tablespoon water. Reduce the heat to medium-low, scrape any brown bits from the bottom of the pan, and cook, stirring occasionally, until golden brown, 8 to 10 minutes more. Stir the mushrooms into the pan for the last 5 minutes and allow them to soften.

3. Add the wine and stir to deglaze the pan, scraping up any browned bits from the bottom. Stir in the parsley and season with salt and pepper. Serve on top of the burger.

CHICKEN ENCHILADAS VERDES

SERVES 6

1 pound tomatillos

1 tablespoon extra-virgin olive oil

½ cup finely diced sweet onion

3 garlic cloves, minced

3 cups low-sodium chicken broth

½ (8-ounce) package cream cheese

½ teaspoon salt

¼ teaspoon freshly ground black pepper

2 cups chopped fresh cilantro, plus 1 tablespoon for garnish

½ to 2 jalapeños (according to heat preference), seeded and diced

4 cups shredded cooked chicken (from 3 or 4 grilled chicken breasts)

1½ cups frozen corn kernels, thawed

1 cup thinly sliced mushrooms

1 teaspoon chili powder

½ teaspoon ground cumin

12 to 14 (6-inch) corn tortilla shells

1 cup crumbled Cotija cheese or queso blanco

1 cup shredded Mexican mixed cheeses (or a mix of cheddar and Monterey Jack)

THIS IS ONE OF MY FAMILY'S FAVORITES, which I can whip up in a jiffy if I'm using a rotisserie chicken. Whenever I serve this enchilada casserole, it is gone within minutes! The salsa verde really makes the enchiladas, and I always cook extra to really soak the enchiladas. And if there is leftover salsa, it's great later in the week on eggs, beans, and of course simply served with tortilla chips.

It looks like a lot of ingredients, but don't let it overwhelm you. This is a really simple enchilada casserole, and if you make it once, you'll get the hang of it. Also, the mushrooms and corn are optional, but I really like getting more nutrition (not to mention flavor) into each enchilada. Even better, use kernels cut from 2 ears of leftover grilled corn in lieu of frozen.

1. Preheat the oven to 350°F.

2. Bring a pot of water to a boil. Dip the tomatillos (husks still on) in the water for a few seconds to soften the husks, then remove from the water. The husks should then easily peel off.

3. In a large saucepan, heat the olive oil over medium heat. Add the onion and cook, stirring, until translucent, about 3 minutes. Add the garlic and cook, stirring, for 1 minute.

4. Pour in the broth and add the tomatillos whole. Boil the tomatillos until they appear to be tender, 6 to 8 minutes

recipe continues

5. Carefully (it's hot!) pour the tomatillos and broth from the pan into a large blender or food processor, working in batches, if necessary. Let cool briefly, then add the cream cheese, salt, and pepper. Give it a quick whir until the tomatillos break down, then add the cilantro and jalapeño and pulse.

6. Pour the salsa back into the saucepan and simmer, allowing the flavors to concentrate a bit, for about 10 minutes.

7. Remove 2 cups of the salsa and set aside, leaving the remaining salsa in the saucepan.

8. Stir the shredded chicken, corn, mushrooms, chili powder, and cumin into the saucepan. Cook, stirring occasionally, until the mushrooms are soft and the chicken absorbs the flavors, 5 to 6 minutes more.

9. Soften and warm the tortillas by sandwiching a few shells between two damp paper towels and microwaving for about 20 seconds.

10. Fill each tortilla shell with 3 to 4 tablespoons of the chicken, mushroom, and corn filling, then roll them. Do not worry if they break a little, as they will still be amazing. Line a 9 by 13-inch baking dish with the rolled enchiladas, squeezing them together as you go.

11. Pour the reserved salsa verde over the top of the enchiladas. Sprinkle the top with the Cotija cheese and then sprinkle on the Mexican shredded cheese. Bake until the cheeses melt, 10 to 12 minutes.

12. Garnish with the rest of the chopped cilantro. Serve right away.

Sides & Salads

VEGGIES, BEANS & GRAINS

This chapter highlights my passion for eating loads of vegetables and healthy grains, such as quinoa. The Incas of the Andes were the first to eat quinoa for the protein and energy it imparts, making it an original superfood. I cook with superfoods whenever I can—for example, I'll substitute chia seeds if a recipe calls for sesame seeds. In fact, I could fill my plate with a few of these dishes every night and be happy (but my boys would never let me neglect their meat proteins).

TOSTONES
(Fried Green Plantains)

GLUTEN-FREE
VEGETARIAN
SERVES 4

1 large green plantain

Vegetable oil, for frying (just enough to coat the bottom of a skillet)

Salt

Note: Serve with salsa or guacamole, black beans and rice, etc…

A TYPE OF LARGE GREEN BANANA you see often next to regular bananas, plantains are not to be overlooked. If you've never had them before, I can understand why they would seem intimidating to cook, but they are as easy to prepare as peeling a potato and frying them up like French fries. Plantains are signature sides in many Latin dishes. They are served mashed (when ripe), in salads, and—my favorite way— as delicious chips perfect for dipping.

In Puerto Rico, I remember my *abuelita* (grandmother) making plantains almost daily. There are lots of fancy ways to prepare them, one of which includes mashing them to chip size. I find a brown grocery bag seems to do the trick. My mother learned the same method from my grandmother. And again, don't let the greenness of the plantain's peel fool you; they are perfect for frying up. When they do start to ripen, like regular bananas, that's when they become sweet and perfect for roasting or mashing, making for a sweet side dish. The traditional preparation of plantains is fried, which is not the healthiest, but you can also bake them in oven (just slice them more thinly using a mandoline and drizzle lightly with olive oil).

1. Remove the thick plantain skin with a knife, then cut the plantains crosswise into ½-inch-thick pieces.

2. In a large skillet, heat enough oil to coat the bottom of the skillet over medium-high heat. Fry the plantains until they are lightly

golden, 2 to 3 minutes on each side. Transfer from the skillet to a paper towel–lined plate and lower the heat (you will return the plantains to the skillet for a second frying after you smash them to chips.)

3. Using a brown grocery bag or waxed paper folded in half (or if you are fancy, you can use a plantain masher or tortilla masher), put a plantain round between the folds, then press the bag down on top, smashing each plantain into a round chip.

4. Add a bit more oil to the skillet if needed, then sprinkle the plantains with salt and return them to the skillet to fry. They're done when they turn golden yellow and crispy. Remove any excess oil by placing them on a paper towel–lined plate.

GREEN PEA MASHED POTATOES with Pesto

GLUTEN-FREE
VEGETARIAN
SERVES 8 TO 10

2 pounds Yukon Gold potatoes (about 4 medium)

1 (12-ounce) bag frozen peas

½ cup buttermilk

Salt and freshly ground black pepper

¼ to ½ cup Easy Pesto (page 161)

Note: You'll have a bit of extra pesto, which is always nice, particularly around the holidays. Spread it on leftover turkey sandwiches, swirl it into tomato soup, make pesto crostini, serve it as a veggie dip, or spoon it on top of a poached egg on toast—you get the idea!

THIS IS A DELICIOUS WAY TO LIGHTEN UP your mashed potatoes while adding flavor and nutrition by swapping some potato with peas. I like to serve this especially during the holidays, as it adds a nice touch of color and is something different from boring white mashed potatoes.

1. Put the potatoes in a large pot and add water to cover. Bring to a boil and boil until they are thoroughly cooked (stick a fork into one if you are unsure—it should be tender), about 15 minutes. Using a slotted spoon and/or tongs, remove the potatoes, let cool slightly, then peel off the skins.

2. Briefly add the peas to same pot of boiling water until they are cooked, about 1 minute. Drain the peas in a colander and put both the potatoes and peas back into the pot.

3. In a small saucepan, warm the buttermilk over medium heat. When hot but not simmering (keep an eye on it), add to the pot with the peas and potatoes.

4. Using a potato masher, mash the potatoes, peas, and buttermilk together (many of the peas will remain intact) and season with salt and pepper.

5. Scoop the mashed potatoes and peas into a serving bowl.

6. Drizzle with ¼ cup (or more to taste) of the pesto in a swirling motion, then using a fork, swirl it throughout so it is lightly incorporated into the potato and pea mash. Serve.

LIGHTENED-UP SWEET POTATO GRATIN

VEGETARIAN
SERVES 8

Vegetable oil, for the baking dish

1 cup low-fat milk

½ cup half-and-half

1 tablespoon all-purpose flour

1 tablespoon unsalted butter

1 tablespoon fresh thyme leaves,
or 2 teaspoons dried

½ teaspoon ground nutmeg

Salt and freshly ground black pepper

¾ cup grated Gruyère cheese

½ cup freshly grated Parmesan cheese

4 medium sweet potatoes, peeled and
sliced very thinly (about ⅛ inch thick), like a
sweet potato chip (a mandoline helps)

½ cup Italian bread crumbs

I LOVE ANYTHING WITH POTATOES AND CHEESE, but we all know how bad that combination is for you, not to mention that there is usually a lot of heavy cream and butter involved as well. So I came up with this sweet potato gratin in an effort to re-create the classic scalloped potato casserole with a lighter touch. Perfect for any occasion, this casserole also makes for a great holiday side or adds just the dose of comfort food you need year-round.

1. Preheat the oven to 400°F. Lightly grease a 4-quart glass lasagna-style baking dish with vegetable oil.

2. In a saucepan, whisk together the milk, half-and-half, flour, butter, thyme, and nutmeg and season with salt and pepper. Heat over medium heat, allowing the milk mixture to thicken slightly, like a looser roux.

3. In a medium bowl, mix the Gruyère and Parmesan cheeses.

4. Arrange the potatoes in tight, thin layers in the prepared baking dish, pouring a bit of the cream mixture over each layer and sprinkling a couple of tablespoons of cheeses on top. Aim for five or six layers and reserve some of the cheese to top the last layer.

5. Top with the reserved cheese, sprinkle with the bread crumbs, and season with salt and pepper. Cover and bake for 30 minutes, then remove the cover and bake until the top browns and a knife inserted into the potatoes comes out easily, 10 to 15 minutes more. Serve.

MUSHROOMS AL AJILLO
(Mushrooms in Garlic Sauce)

GLUTEN-FREE
VEGETARIAN
SERVES 4 TO 6

¼ cup extra-virgin olive oil

1 shallot, minced

2 large garlic cloves, minced

1 pound fresh white or cremini mushrooms, cleaned and stem ends trimmed, halved or quartered if large

¼ cup dry white wine or sherry

Salt and freshly ground black pepper

Handful of fresh parsley, chopped

THIS IS A CLASSIC SIDE STRAIGHT FROM SPAIN, known as *champiñones al ajillo*. I like to serve the mushrooms on the side as an accompaniment to a great steak or pork chop, or serve them tapas-style, with a fresh piece of rustic bread to soak up the garlic sauce. It really is the easiest dish and requires no time to make. It's best to prepare it right before serving.

1. In a large skillet, heat the olive oil over medium-high heat. Add the shallot and cook, stirring, until translucent, about 2 minutes. In the last 15 seconds, stir the garlic and cook, stirring to prevent burning, until fragrant.

2. Add the mushrooms and cook, stirring, until they are slightly tender, about 4 minutes.

3. Add the wine and cook, stirring frequently, until the wine has mostly cooked off, 4 to 5 minutes more. Season with salt and pepper.

4. Pour it all (including whatever liquid is left) onto a serving platter and garnish with the parsley.

KALE &
Collard Greens

GLUTEN-FREE
VEGETARIAN
SERVES 4

2 tablespoons extra-virgin olive oil

2 garlic cloves, minced

1 cup packed chopped fresh
collard green leaves

2 tablespoons fresh lemon juice
or apple cider vinegar

1 cup packed chopped fresh kale leaves

Salt and freshly ground black pepper

Toasted pine nuts (see Tip) for added
crunch or cooked bacon bits for flavor
(optional)

Tip: To toast pine nuts, put the nuts
in a dry, nonstick skillet over medium-
low heat. Cook, stirring frequently,
until lightly browned, about
3 minutes.

ALL HAIL KALE AND COLLARD GREENS. This super greens combination packs a punch of nutrition and filling flavor. It's so easy to make this side; plan on no more than 5 minutes total prep and cooking time. Make it right before serving so it goes straight from the pan to your plate, as it goes cold quickly.

1. In a deep skillet, heat the olive oil over medium heat. Add the garlic and cook quickly, stirring, until the garlic becomes fragrant, about 30 seconds.

2. Stir in the collard greens first, as they take a bit longer to cook. Add ¼ cup water and the lemon juice and cook, stirring continuously, until the collards are slightly wilted and tender but still green, about 3 minutes.

3. Stir in the kale, mix well, and cook until the leaves are wilted halfway but still green, about 2 minutes more. Remove from the heat so they don't overcook and become brown.

4. Season with salt and pepper and top with toasted pine nuts, if desired. Serve right away.

KALE PESTO SPAGHETTI SQUASH

GLUTEN-FREE
VEGETARIAN
SERVES 6 TO 8

KALE PESTO

1 bunch kale, stemmed, leaves
chopped (about 2 cups)

½ cup chopped fresh basil

2 tablespoons pine nuts

2 garlic cloves

½ cup extra-virgin olive oil

½ cup freshly grated Parmesan cheese,
plus more for serving (optional)

Salt

SQUASH

1 large spaghetti squash (about 5 pounds)

Salt and freshly ground black pepper

¼ cup extra-virgin olive oil

THIS IS MY GUILT-FREE WAY TO SATISFY MY PASTA CRAVING, while also getting a nutritious boost from all the vegetables. Of course nothing is quite like pasta and pesto or marinara sauce, but this mild-tasting, tender squash is a worthy replacement. You can try the spaghetti squash with a traditional marinara or Turkey Bolognese (page 105), if you prefer.

I like to cook spaghetti squash on the weekend and store it in the refrigerator. Then, during the week when I'm rushed for time, I top it with the sauce of my choosing and voilà! It's a healthy and surprisingly filling meal.

1. Preheat the oven to 450°F.

2. **Make the kale pesto:** In a food processor, combine the kale, basil, pine nuts, and garlic and process until finely chopped. With the motor running, drizzle in the olive oil in a thin stream. Add the Parmesan last and process until the pesto is smooth. Season with salt.

3. **Make the squash:** To make it easier to cut, microwave the spaghetti squash whole to soften, turning once, for about 5 minutes. Cut it in half lengthwise and remove the seeds (keep the seeds for later, if you like—they roast just like pumpkin seeds!).

4. Season the inside of the squash halves with salt and pepper and coat with the olive oil. Bake on a baking sheet, cut-side down, until tender and easily pierced through to the skin with a fork, about 45 minutes. Remove from the oven and let it cool.

5. Using a large fork, scrape out the inside of the spaghetti squash "noodles," using long strokes in line with the threads of the squash to create the longest strands. Throw away the outer skin. To remove some of the extra water, drain the "noodles" using a colander (similar to pasta) for several minutes.

6. Toss in a large bowl with enough kale pesto to coat all the "noodles." Season with salt and pepper, and sprinkle with additional Parmesan, if you like. Serve warm or cold.

SOUTHWESTERN QUINOA BLACK BEAN SALAD

GLUTEN-FREE
VEGETARIAN
SERVES 6 TO 8

2 cups cooked quinoa (prepared according to the package instructions)

2 (15-ounce) cans black beans, drained and rinsed

2 ears corn, roasted or grilled, or 2 cups frozen corn kernels, thawed

½ cup diced red bell pepper

3 green onions, thinly sliced

¼ cup chopped fresh cilantro, plus 1 tablespoon for garnish

¼ cup chopped fresh parsley

3 tablespoons extra-virgin olive oil

2 tablespoons fresh lemon juice

1 teaspoon Tajín chili lime spice (or make your own using ½ teaspoon chili powder, ¼ teaspoon garlic salt, and ¼ teaspoon grated lime zest)

Salt and freshly ground black pepper

1 ripe avocado

1 cup chopped grilled chicken, for added protein (optional)

ONCE AGAIN, MY FAVORITE GRAIN, QUINOA, IS THE STAR OF THIS QUICKIE SIDE. There is very little in the way of cooking or prep here if you've made your quinoa ahead of time. To make it a meal, add shredded grilled chicken or beef and fresh avocado upon serving.

1. In a large bowl, toss together the quinoa, beans, corn, bell pepper, green onions, ¼ cup of the cilantro, and the parsley.

2. In a small bowl, whisk together the olive oil, lemon juice, Tajín spice, and salt and pepper to taste. Drizzle the vinaigrette over the salad and toss to distribute.

3. When ready to serve, test the seasoning and add more salt and pepper, if needed. Pit, peel, and dice the avocado and arrange it on top of the salad. Serve topped with chicken, if desired, and garnished with the remaining cilantro.

CLASSIC BRAZILIAN BLACK BEANS
& Rice

GLUTEN-FREE
VEGETARIAN
SERVES 8 TO 10

1 tablespoon extra-virgin olive oil

1 green or red bell pepper, diced

1 cup chopped yellow onion

2 garlic cloves, minced

2 (16-ounce) cans black beans, drained and rinsed

1 tablespoon red wine vinegar or sherry vinegar

1 teaspoon minced fresh oregano, or ½ teaspoon dried

½ teaspoon ground cumin

¼ teaspoon cayenne pepper

Splash of Tabasco sauce

Salt and freshly ground black pepper

Fresh cilantro, for garnish

Brazilian White Rice (recipe follows)

IF THERE IS ONE DISH THAT DEFINES ME, IT WOULD BE BLACK BEANS AND RICE. It's the meal I ate most often as a child (with Puerto Rican and Brazilian family) and continues to be one of my favorites served on the side or on its own served with a salad. Beans and rice is the heart and soul of Caribbean and South American cuisine brought to this part of the world through the slave trade. It was considered peasant food, but an essential replacement to expensive meat. Now every region has its own style of preparation and preference of bean (black, pinto, red) but any way it is served, it's good food for the soul.

To prepare this dish the easy way, open up a can of black beans, add simple seasonings and flavors, and serve it with rice. You can also use dried beans (soak them overnight first, then boil in fresh water for 1 hour), but there is no real flavor difference when you use canned, and it is so much faster. Because I grew up eating lots of beans, I like to make a batch almost every week and I will use them throughout the week in burritos and salads, or reheat them for a simple and fast lunch on the go.

1. In a soup pot, heat the olive oil over medium-high heat. Add the bell pepper and onion and cook, stirring, until the onion begins to soften, about 3 minutes. Add the garlic and cook, stirring to making sure it doesn't burn, for another minute.

2. Stir in the beans, vinegar, oregano, cumin, cayenne, and Tabasco. Reduce the heat to low, cover, and simmer until slightly thickened, 5 minutes more. Season with salt and black pepper.

3. Garnish with fresh cilantro and serve on top of Brazilian White Rice.

BRAZILIAN WHITE RICE

GLUTEN-FREE
VEGETARIAN
SERVES 8

1 tablespoon extra-virgin olive oil

2 garlic cloves, minced

2 cups long-grain white rice
(I prefer jasmine rice)

1 teaspoon salt

Chopped fresh cilantro,
for garnish

COOKING WHITE RICE IS NOT AS EASY AS IT SOUNDS. You know what I mean if you've had it burn or get too sticky or gooey. So I know you are asking, "What's the difference with Brazilian white rice?" There is plenty, and it all comes down to flavor, texture, and preparation. My mom makes the absolute best white rice, which smells amazing and like home. Her secret: She cooks the raw rice grains in bacon fat and garlic for a minute or two. My approach is a bit healthier and uses olive oil, but it still tastes just as delicious. I have made it using long-grain brown rice instead, and it works just as well. You will never go back to mushy, bland, or too-sticky white rice again once you try this.

1. In a large pot, heat the olive oil over medium heat. Add the garlic and cook, stirring to make sure it doesn't burn, until it is translucent, about 1 minute.

2. Stir in the rice and salt and cook, stirring to coat the grains with the oil and garlic, for about 2 minutes.

3. Pour in 3 cups water and cover the pot. Reduce the heat to low. Check the rice every 5 minutes or so to make sure there is still water and it hasn't been fully absorbed prematurely.

4. Let the rice simmer for about 15 minutes, then check it again. It will likely be a little al dente. If the water has been fully absorbed, add another ½ cup and cook, covered, for 5 to 10 minutes more. After 20 to 25 minutes total cooking time, it should be tender and fluffy and the water should be fully absorbed.

5. When done, remove the rice pot from the burner and let it sit, still covered, for 5 minutes more. Fluff the rice with a fork and garnish with cilantro.

COCONUT RICE

GLUTEN-FREE
VEGETARIAN
SERVES 6 TO 8

2 tablespoons coconut oil

2 cups long-grain white rice
(I prefer jasmine rice)

1 cup unsweetened coconut milk

1 teaspoon salt

3 tablespoons unsweetened coconut flakes

1 tablespoon chopped fresh cilantro
(optional)

Note: Serve Coconut Rice as the perfect partner to my Salmon with Sesame-Soy-Ginger Glaze (page 166) or try it with Crispy Shrimp with Mango-Pineapple Soy Sauce (page 157) or Chicken Korma Kebabs (page 100). And since this recipe comes straight from Brazil, where they love coconut rice with seafood stews using coconut milk, you'll never go wrong pairing this with my Bahian Cod Fillet (page 163).

WANT TO TAKE YOUR PLAIN WHITE RICE UP A NOTCH? This coconut rice is a wonderful complement to fish, shrimp, or chicken made with tropical flavors—and can cool down the heat of spicy foods. It adds the right amount of sweetness and nuttiness, along with the tang of citrus through the fresh lime zest and cilantro.

1. In a rice pot or saucepan, heat the coconut oil over medium heat. Add the rice and stir until all the grains are coated with oil.

2. Add 1½ cups water, the coconut milk, and the salt. Stir, then cover and reduce the heat to low. Simmer for about 15 minutes, checking periodically to make sure the liquids haven't cooked off entirely and that the rice isn't burning on the bottom. It will likely be a little al dente. If the water has been fully absorbed, add another ½ cup and cook, covered, until tender and fluffy and the water has been fully absorbed, 5 to 10 minutes more.

3. Stir in the coconut flakes and fluff the rice with a fork. Remove from the heat and let sit, covered, for 5 minutes.

4. Serve garnished with the cilantro, if desired.

SALADS & SOUPS

HORIATIKI
(Classic Greek Salad)

GLUTEN-FREE
VEGETARIAN
SERVES 4

DRESSING

½ cup extra-virgin olive oil

¼ cup fresh lemon juice

1 teaspoon red wine vinegar

1 garlic clove, pressed

1 teaspoon minced fresh oregano,
or ¼ teaspoon dried

1 teaspoon minced fresh dill,
or ¼ teaspoon dried

1 tablespoon finely crumbled feta cheese

1 tablespoon minced kalamata olives

Salt and freshly ground black pepper

SALAD

4 large ripe heirloom or plum tomatoes,
cored and chopped into chunks

1 medium head romaine lettuce,
cut into bite-size pieces

1 medium cucumber, peeled, seeded,
and chopped into chunks

1 green bell pepper, chopped into chunks

½ red onion, very thinly sliced

½ cup coarsely chopped kalamata
or black olives

½ cup crumbled feta cheese

ONE OF MY FAVORITE ASSIGNMENTS: going to the Olympics. Aside from enjoying all the amazing competition and getting to know the athletes, I love getting to spend time in a country and really learn about its culture and people and sample its food and drink. My passion for the Greek salad and anything Greek cuisine comes from my very first Olympics at the *TODAY* show in Athens in 2004. My diet there included a healthy, heaping Greek salad just about every day. It's so simple, yet delicious and fresh. There is something about those Greek tomatoes, I tell you, that makes them taste like candy! Maybe it's the hot, dry climate, the rocky soil—who knows? Regardless, I was hooked, and have made it one of my go-to salad recipes.

1. **Make the dressing:** In a small bowl, whisk together the olive oil, lemon juice, vinegar, garlic, oregano, and dill. Stir in the feta and olives and season with salt and black pepper. Set aside and only dress the salad right before serving.

2. **Make the salad:** In a large salad bowl, toss together the tomatoes, romaine, cucumber, bell pepper, onion, and olives.

3. When ready to serve, top with the feta cheese, drizzle in the dressing, and toss well.

Variation

JUST PEACHY SUMMER SALAD

What to do with all those delicious summer peaches? I like this combination, with a classic Greek salad twist. Here you have the most delicious taste of summer. Don't have peaches? Try watermelon, as feta and watermelon are a match made in heaven.

1. Combine a couple of thinly sliced pitted peaches, chopped heirloom or other summer tomatoes, a handful of crumbled feta, some sliced red onion, cucumbers, bell peppers, and radish.

2. When ready to serve, top with the Greek salad dressing and garnish with fresh mint.

GRILLED SUMMER VEGETABLE PLATTER

GLUTEN-FREE
VEGETARIAN
SERVES 4 TO 6

1 medium eggplant, cut into
¼-inch-thick rounds

½ bunch asparagus, ends trimmed

1 yellow squash, cut lengthwise into
⅛-inch-thick slices

1 zucchini, cut lengthwise
into ⅛-inch-thick slices

1 red bell pepper,
cut into 2-inch-thick slices

3 ears sweet corn

20 to 25 cremini mushrooms, washed,
stems trimmed but left on

1 red onion, cut into ¼-inch-thick rounds

⅓ cup extra-virgin olive oil

3 tablespoons balsamic vinegar

1 teaspoon fresh thyme leaves

1 teaspoon minced fresh oregano

Coarse sea salt and freshly ground
black pepper

Marinated mozzarella or goat cheese balls
(optional)

NOW THAT I'M IN CALIFORNIA, I love shopping at the local farmers' market and using whatever is in season, particularly when making an all-vegetable dish like this one. My favorite colorful combination includes summer squash, zucchini, red bell pepper, eggplant, asparagus, mushrooms, red onion, and maybe summer corn, cut into smaller pieces. Try it out next time you entertain and need something simple and elegant . . . and stress-free. You can grill it all ahead of time, as it's as good at room temperature as it is right off the grill.

1. Put the eggplant, asparagus, squash, zucchini, bell pepper, corn, mushrooms, and onion in a large, resealable plastic bag. In a small bowl, whisk together the olive oil, vinegar, thyme, and oregano. Reserve 3 tablespoons of the marinade and pour the rest into the bag with the vegetables. Seal it and allow the veggies to marinate at room temperature for 1 hour.

2. Heat a grill to medium, around 350°F on a temperature gauge.

3. Remove the vegetables from the marinade and season them with salt and black pepper. Thread the mushrooms onto two skewers.

4. Put the corn on the grill first. Rotate it after you develop a nice grill mark, about 3 minutes on each side. Remove and, when cool, cut each ear into three or four pieces.

5. Add the eggplant, squash, zucchini, bell pepper, asparagus, mushrooms, and onion to the grill, in batches if necessary. Flip or

Note: This recipe requires 1 hour of marinating.

rotate, removing them as they develop a nice char: about 4 minutes for the onions and asparagus; 6 to 7 minutes for the squash, zucchini, eggplant, and mushrooms; and about 8 minutes for the bell pepper.

6. On a large serving platter, arrange all the vegetables in a layered design and serve topped with mozzarella, if desired. Drizzle the vegetables with the reserved marinade and season with salt and black pepper. Serve warm or room temperature.

TABLESIDE CAESAR SALAD

SERVES 4 TO 6

1 large egg yolk

1 tablespoons fresh lemon juice

½ teaspoon Worcestershire sauce

½ teaspoon dry mustard

¼ cup extra-virgin olive oil

2 large garlic cloves (more or less, depending on how garlicky you like it), pressed

½ teaspoon anchovy paste (optional)

Splash of Tabasco sauce

Salt

4 romaine lettuce hearts, chopped into bite-size chunks

¼ cup freshly grated Parmesan cheese

Herbed Croutons (recipe follows)

Freshly ground black pepper

I LOVE ORDERING A TABLESIDE CAESAR SALAD at restaurants and watching them make it fresh. It's good dinner theater. You can give your guests or family that same tableside service, guaranteed to impress. Now, my husband is not a fan of anchovies, but a tiny little bit will do, and he doesn't even know the difference. Add some sliced grilled chicken for a more complete meal.

1. Just before serving, make this tableside: In a glass bowl, whisk together the egg yolk, lemon juice, Worcestershire, and dry mustard. While whisking, drizzle in the olive oil in a thin stream, whisking to emulsify.

2. Whisk in the garlic, anchovy paste (if using), and Tabasco. Season with salt, particularly if you're not using the anchovy paste.

3. Toss the dressing with the romaine, then sprinkle with the grated Parmesan. Serve topped with Herbed Croutons and seasoned with pepper.

HERBED CROUTONS

½ loaf day-old whole wheat bread, cut into
½- to 1-inch cubes (3 to 4 cups)

2 teaspoons fresh thyme leaves,
or ¼ teaspoon dried

2 teaspoons minced fresh oregano,
or ¼ teaspoon dried

Salt

¼ cup extra-virgin olive oil

1. Preheat the oven to 375°F.

2. In a large bowl, toss the bread cubes with the thyme, oregano, and salt to taste. Drizzle in the olive oil and toss to coat.

3. Spread the croutons out onto a large rimmed baking sheet and bake until golden and crisp, about 10 minutes. Serve immediately or store in an airtight container at room temperature for 1 to 2 days.

FRENCH ONION SOUP

2 tablespoons unsalted butter

4 medium onions, cut into ⅛-inch-thick slices

1 teaspoon sugar

1 tablespoon all-purpose flour

2 (14-ounce) cans beef broth (3½ cups)

½ cup dry white wine

2 garlic cloves, pressed

1 teaspoon Worcestershire sauce

2 sprigs fresh thyme, or 1 teaspoon dried thyme leaves

1 bay leaf

Salt and freshly ground black pepper

6 to 8 (½-inch-thick) slices French bread

1 cup shredded Gruyère cheese

Note: You can make the soup ahead of time or even days in advance, just refrigerate then reheat, but finish with the bread and cheese right before serving.

ONE OF MY FAVORITE SOUPS OF ALL TIME, nothing smells more fragrant or is more cozy then a heaping bowl of French onion soup on a crisp fall day. The key to really making it taste just as good as any restaurant's is to take the time to caramelize the onions. You want the onions to melt in your mouth like butter. Bake the cheese until golden on top and serve the soup in individual French onion soup crocks.

1. In a Dutch oven, melt the butter over medium-low heat. Add the onions and sugar and cook, stirring frequently, to let the onions caramelize, about 30 minutes.

2. Sprinkle in the flour and stir for 1 minute to thicken. Stir in the broth, 1 cup water, the wine, garlic, Worcestershire, thyme, and bay leaf and season with salt and pepper. Simmer, uncovered, until the broth is reduced and rich tasting, about 30 minutes.

3. Toast the French bread slices until golden on both sides.

4. Set the oven to broil. Dole the soup out into the ramekins or crocks, removing the bay leaf and thyme sprigs. Put a slice of French bread in each crock, then sprinkle the tops liberally with the Gruyère. Broil until the cheese melts and becomes golden on the edges. Serve immediately.

COCONUT CHICKEN CURRY SOUP

GLUTEN-FREE
SERVES 4 TO 6

2 tablespoons extra-virgin olive oil

1 small yellow onion, minced (about 1 cup)

2 tablespoons plus 2 teaspoons curry powder, or 1 tablespoon red curry paste

1 garlic clove, pressed

4 chicken breasts (about 1½ pounds), very thinly sliced

4 cups chicken broth

1 (15-ounce) can light coconut milk

2 tablespoons fresh lime juice, plus lime wedges for garnish

1 tablespoon dark brown sugar

¼ teaspoon ground turmeric

1 medium red bell pepper, thinly sliced

1 cup thinly sliced mushrooms

Salt

2 green onions, thinly sliced into rings

¼ cup chopped fresh cilantro

¼ cup chopped fresh peanuts, for garnish (optional)

THAI FOOD IS A CUISINE I CRAVE, and this soup tops my Thai food list. It combines two of my favorite flavors when cooking, coconut and curry, and delivers a bit of a kick. It may seem exotic and therefore most might think difficult to make, but rest assured that this will take you no more than 30 minutes and is a really good first course or even lunch.

1. In a stockpot, heat the olive oil over medium heat. Add the onion and cook, stirring, until it softens but does not brown, reducing the heat if necessary, 3 to 5 minutes.

2. Stir in the curry and garlic, then add the chicken and cook lightly, stirring, for about 2 minutes.

3. Add the broth, coconut milk, lime juice, brown sugar, and turmeric and bring to a boil, allowing the chicken to cook further, about 5 minutes.

4. Stir in the bell pepper and mushrooms and simmer until the vegetables are cooked, 2 to 3 minutes more. Season with salt.

5. Ladle into bowls and top with green onions, cilantro, and chopped peanuts, if desired. Garnish with a slice of lime on the side.

POTATO, COLLARD GREEN & CHICKPEA SOUP with Italian Sausage

GLUTEN-FREE
SERVES 6

3 (6-inch) links sweet or spicy Italian sausage, cut into ¼- to ½-inch slices

1 tablespoon extra-virgin olive oil

2 cups diced yellow onion

1 cup thinly sliced leek

3 garlic cloves, minced

2 (15-ounce) cans chickpeas, drained and rinsed

28 ounces chicken broth (3½ cups)

1 cup diced peeled white potato (½-inch cubes)

1 Goya ham flavoring packet (or put a ham hock in the broth, just for flavoring)

1 bay leaf

2 cups chopped collard green or kale leaves

Salt and freshly ground black pepper

THE INSPIRATION FOR THIS RECIPE comes from *caldo gallego* soup, which I had many times growing up in Spain. This is a traditional soup served up in Spain's northwest corner, Galicia, which can be a little rainy and cold; thus, it's the perfect soul-warming soup. I altered the traditional soup by using chickpeas instead of white beans and Italian sausage instead of chorizo, along with a few other little twists.

1. In a large pot, fry the sausage over medium heat until golden on both sides, about 5 minutes. Add the olive oil, then add the onion, leek, and garlic and cook, stirring, until the onion has softened, about 3 minutes.

2. Add the chickpeas, broth, potato, 1 cup water, the ham flavoring, and the bay leaf. Stir and cover. Cook until the potatoes are tender, 10 to 15 minutes. Stir in the collard greens and cook just until the greens are wilted, 3 to 5 minutes more.

3. Season with salt and pepper, remove the bay leaf, and serve.

MUSHROOM & BARLEY VEGETARIAN SOUP

VEGETARIAN
SERVES 8 TO 10

1 tablespoon extra-virgin olive oil

2 cups chopped yellow onion

1 cup diced carrots

½ cup diced celery

1 pound fresh mushrooms, cleaned, ends trimmed, and sliced

2 garlic cloves, minced

1 tablespoon tomato paste

1½ teaspoons fresh thyme leaves, or ½ teaspoon dried

28 ounces vegetable broth (3½ cups)

½ cup barley (medium pearl preferred)

1 tablespoon Worcestershire sauce

1 teaspoon smoked paprika

1 bay leaf

½ teaspoon salt

¼ teaspoon freshly ground black pepper

2 tablespoons chopped fresh parsley, for garnish

HERE'S A SOUP THAT TRULY WARMS THE SOUL and is oh so good for you, too. Most mushroom and barley soups are made with beef and beef broth. I made it my own in this vegetarian version—it still has the same robust flavors, without the meat.

1. In a large stockpot or Dutch oven, heat the olive oil over medium-high heat. Add the onion, carrots, and celery and cook, stirring, until they start to become tender, about 3 minutes.

2. Add the mushrooms, garlic, tomato paste, and thyme and cook, stirring frequently, until the mushrooms release their moisture, about 3 minutes.

3. Stir in the broth, 1 cup water, the barley, Worcestershire, paprika, bay leaf, salt, and pepper. Bring the soup to a boil, then reduce the heat to low, cover, and simmer until the barley is tender, about 1½ hours.

4. Remove the bay leaf before serving. Adjust the seasoning with salt and pepper, if needed. Sprinkle the soup with the parsley upon serving.

TOMATO-EGGPLANT COULIS, SUNNY-SIDE UP

VEGETARIAN
SERVES 4 TO 6

2 to 3 tablespoons extra-virgin olive oil, plus more as needed

1 eggplant, cut into 1-inch cubes

½ medium yellow onion, diced

2 garlic cloves, minced

1 zucchini, chopped

1 cup chopped fresh mushrooms

Red pepper flakes

Salt

1 (28-ounce) can diced tomatoes with juices

2 tablespoons chopped fresh basil

1 tablespoon minced fresh oregano, or 1 teaspoon dried

Freshly ground black pepper

2 to 3 teaspoons sugar (optional)

4 to 6 large eggs (1 egg per serving)

4 to 6 tablespoons freshly grated Parmesan cheese (1 tablespoon per serving)

Sourdough or French bread slices, for serving

Note: For a more robust meal, use to top fresh pasta, couscous, rice, or even chicken cutlets and finish with a sprinkle of Parmesan cheese.

THIS IS NOT REALLY A SOUP, but rather a hearty tomato-and-eggplant stew served with a perfectly cooked sunny-side-up egg on top, like they serve in France. I came up with this one day when I had a lot of sauce left over from making chicken Parmesan. That week, for lunch, I decided to heat some of the sauce in a ramekin and pair it with a hunk of fresh bread and an egg on top, and I was in heaven. It's perfectly healthy and versatile.

1. In a large stockpot or Dutch oven, heat 2 tablespoons of the olive oil over medium-high heat. Add the eggplant and cook, stirring continuously, until it starts to soften, about 2 minutes. If the eggplant starts to stick, add a third tablespoon of the oil.

2. Stir in the onion and garlic and cook, stirring, until the eggplant is golden brown, about 2 minutes. Add the zucchini and mushrooms and cook, stirring, until they are somewhat tender, 2 to 3 minutes. Season with red pepper flakes and salt.

3. Add the tomatoes and their juices, basil, and oregano and simmer, partially covered, until it thickens, about 20 minutes; after about 10 minutes, taste and check the seasoning; add salt, pepper, or a bit of sugar, if needed.

4. In a skillet coated with olive oil, fry the eggs individually, sunny-side up, over medium heat until the whites are cooked but the yolks are still runny.

5. Spoon the tomato coulis into individual ramekins, putting an egg on top of each serving. Sprinkle each dish with 1 tablespoon of the Parmesan and serve with crusty fresh bread slices on the side.

20-MINUTE GAZPACHO

VEGETARIAN
SERVES 8 TO 10
(½ CUP SERVINGS)

1 (28-ounce) can whole San Marzano tomatoes with juices

½ cup sherry wine vinegar

¼ cup extra-virgin olive oil

½ small yellow onion, chopped

1 red bell pepper, ½ coarsely chopped, ½ finely diced and reserved for garnish

1 cucumber, ½ coarsely chopped, ½ finely diced and reserved for garnish

1 teaspoon minced fresh thyme, or ½ teaspoon dried

1 teaspoon minced fresh oregano, or ½ teaspoon dried

Dash of Tabasco sauce

Salt and freshly ground black pepper

1 avocado, pitted, peeled, and diced, for garnish

Chopped fresh cilantro, for garnish

Herbed Croutons (page 229)

GAZPACHO IS ONE OF MY MOST-REQUESTED, signature recipes, picked up from my years in Spain. A small cup of this refreshing soup is the first thing served at most meals in Spain, like their version of a first-course salad. The acid of the tomato opens up your taste buds. It is so easy to make, honestly, I quite often improv… adding seasonal fruits like watermelon or even peaches, and topping it off with fresh avocado and crab. It's like summer in a bowl, but because it starts with high-quality canned tomatoes, you can make it year-round.

Here is the basic recipe, which you can of course add to with those aforementioned summer flavors.

1. In a large blender, working in batches if necessary, puree the tomatoes and their juices, vinegar, and olive oil. Add the onion, and coarsely chopped bell pepper, and coarsely chopped cucumber. Add the thyme, oregano, Tabasco, and salt and black pepper to taste and puree until smooth. Taste and correct the seasonings if necessary. It should be tangy. If needed, add more vinegar or olive oil. Refrigerate until fully chilled.

2. When you're ready to serve, bring out the gazpacho. (The colder you serve it, the better!) Garnish with the finely diced bell pepper, finely diced cucumber, avocado, and cilantro, and then top with the Herbed Croutons.

Weekend Brunch

On the weekends that we're all able to take the morning off (i.e., there are no soccer games to rush off to), we love to spend time as a family, cooking and sharing our latest and greatest news. We're always making loads of variations based on cravings and what the refrigerator yields, but these are some of the most popular brunch picks. I can almost smell that banana bread now, fresh out of the oven.

TORTILLA ESPAÑOLA

GLUTEN-FREE
VEGETARIAN
SERVES 6 TO 8

3 tablespoons extra-virgin olive oil

2 medium yellow onions, thinly sliced

1 garlic clove, minced

1 large Yukon Gold potato, peeled and very thinly sliced

1 teaspoon smoked paprika

Salt and freshly ground black pepper

½ green bell pepper, thinly sliced, then chopped

6 large eggs

1 tablespoon minced fresh basil leaves

⅓ cup chopped fresh parsley

IN SPAIN YOU CAN FIND wedges of this egg-and-potato cake at breakfast, lunch, cocktails, or dinner. It's most widely served as an appetizer, but you can have it out all day for your family to snack on, as it's best served room temperature. In Spain they'll even serve it on a baguette or roll to make a *bocadillo*—just take a chunk of bread, slide in a slice of tortilla, and you have an egg-and-potato sandwich: a classic *merienda*, or daytime snack. I like it served with a dash of Tabasco or spoonful of salsa, and it makes good leftovers, too.

1. In a large nonstick sauté pan, heat 1 tablespoon of the olive oil over medium heat. Add the onions and cook, stirring continuously, until translucent, about 5 minutes. Add the garlic and cook, stirring continuously, until fragrant, about 30 seconds. Set the onion and garlic aside.

2. In the same pan, heat another tablespoon of the olive oil over medium heat. Add the potato slices and cook, flipping them occasionally, until translucent and tender but not soft or browned, about 8 minutes; lower the heat if they are cooking too quickly and starting to brown. Season with the paprika and salt and black pepper to taste.

3. Add the bell pepper and cook, stirring occasionally, until starting to soften, about 2 minutes more. Remove the pan from the heat and stir the onions and garlic into the potato mixture.

recipe continues

4. In large bowl, beat the eggs with the basil. Season with salt and black pepper. Stir the potato-onion mixture into the eggs.

5. In a 6- to 8-inch omelet pan (or a double-sided nonstick frittata pan), heat the remaining 1 tablespoon olive oil over medium heat. Add the potato-onion mixture to the pan and cover. When the eggs appear somewhat golden on the bottom and not too runny on top, about 5 minutes, sprinkle the parsley over the tortilla. Flip and cook the other side, uncovered, until golden, 2 to 3 minutes more.

6. Place a plate on top of the pan and invert quickly to flip the tortilla onto the plate. Serve in wedges, hot or at room temperature.

CREPES: SWEET & SAVORY

VEGETARIAN
MAKES 15 TO 20
CREPES

2 tablespoons plus 2 teaspoons
unsalted butter

2 large eggs

2 cups whole or 2% milk

3 tablespoons sugar (optional)

½ teaspoon pure vanilla extract (optional)

1½ cups all-purpose flour

1 teaspoon baking powder

¼ teaspoon salt

Notes: For the most consistent crepe making, it helps to let the batter rest for at least 2 hours before cooking, or to refrigerate it overnight. • You can refrigerate cooked crepes for up to 2 days, then warm them in the microwave for a quick 45 seconds, keeping them covered to seal in the moisture.

AS EITHER A WEEKEND BRUNCH FAVORITE OR A DESSERT, the great thing is you can make crepes and then refrigerate them until you're ready to serve. Dress them up with bananas, strawberries, crème fraîche, or my kids' favorite: Nutella with strawberries, dusted with powdered sugar. Personally, I prefer crepes with eggs, mushrooms, ham, sautéed spinach, and Swiss cheese. There are just so many ways to serve crepes, so let's get started.

1. In a small saucepan, melt 2 tablespoons of the butter over low heat (or "zap" them for 20 seconds in a microwaveable bowl); set aside.

2. In a large bowl, whisk or beat the eggs for 1 minute, then whisk in the milk and, if you are making sweet crepes, the sugar and vanilla.

3. In another large bowl, whisk together the flour, baking powder, and salt.

4. Make a well in the dry ingredients, then pour in the milk mixture, beating with a hand mixer until smooth and not lumpy. Stir in the melted butter and mix until evenly incorporated. For ideal consistency, rest the batter for about 2 hours before cooking, or refrigerate the batter overnight and cook the crepes the next day.

5. Heat a 6- or 8-inch nonstick skillet over medium-high heat. When it is very hot, melt the remaining 2 teaspoons butter. Pour

recipe continues

about 3 tablespoons of the batter into the pan and swirl so that it coats the pan in a thin layer. Cook until the edges curl up a bit, about 1 minute. Flip the crepe with a spatula and brown the other side for another minute. Transfer to a plate and cook the remainder of the batter, stacking up the crepes on the plate as you go. Cover the crepes with another plate and wrap in a plastic bag to keep them from drying out or hardening.

Variations

SWEET CREPES

Strawberry/Banana Cream Crepes: Whip 1 cup heavy cream with 1 tablespoon sugar and ½ teaspoon vanilla extract until it holds stiff peaks. Thinly slice strawberries or bananas. Spoon 1 to 2 tablespoons of the whipped cream into the center of the crepes and layer it with strawberry and banana slices. Fold the crepe in half, then in half again, forming a triangle. Serve with a sprinkle of powdered sugar on top.

Nutella Crepes: Substitute 1 tablespoon Nutella for the whipped cream, spread thinly over the crepe, and then layer on the strawberries and bananas.

SAVORY CREPES

Here's my favorite: Over low heat, scramble 1 beaten egg with a tablespoon milk. Heat 1 tablespoon olive oil and sauté 1 cup spinach leaves and ¼ cup thinly sliced mushrooms (any kind is fine). Season with a pinch each of salt and pepper. Make sure the crepe is still warm, then spread the egg, spinach, and mushrooms over the crepe and layer with Swiss or mozzarella cheese. Fold the crepe in half, then again in half to form a triangle, and serve. For an added kick, serve with a side of hot sauce.

VEGGIE FRITTATA

GLUTEN-FREE
VEGETARIAN
SERVES 6 TO 8

8 large eggs

¼ cup skim milk

1 teaspoon fresh thyme leaves,
or ¼ teaspoon dried

1 teaspoon minced fresh oregano,
or ¼ teaspoon dried

½ teaspoon salt

Pinch of freshly ground black pepper

1 cup shredded mozzarella cheese

2 tablespoons extra-virgin olive oil

½ cup diced yellow onion

½ cup diced mushrooms

¾ cup diced zucchini

¾ cup diced broccoli florets,
or ½ cup chopped spinach

¼ cup freshly grated Parmesan cheese

A FRITTATA IS LIKE A CRUSTLESS QUICHE that makes for a delicious weekend brunch meal that can be both vegetarian and gluten-free. It's a good dish for using up any vegetables you have, too (feel free to add or substitute with vegetables of your choice). If you do like a little more substance and want a meatier meal, add some cooked low-fat turkey sausage. I make this when I have family or friends visiting during the holidays. It's quick and easy, and the best part? It works as breakfast, lunch, or even as a light dinner.

1. Preheat the oven to 350°F.

2. In a large bowl, whisk together the eggs, milk, thyme, oregano, salt, and pepper. Stir in the mozzarella and set aside.

3. In a 9-inch cast-iron or other oven-safe skillet, heat 1 table-spoon of the olive oil over medium heat. Add the onion and mushrooms and cook, stirring, until the onion begins to soften, about 3 minutes. Stir in the zucchini and broccoli, evenly distributing the vegetables. Pour the egg mixture into the skillet and transfer to the oven.

4. Bake until the eggs are cooked firm and the top is golden, about 35 minutes. When 5 minutes remain, top with the Parmesan.

HUEVOS RANCHEROS

VEGETARIAN
SERVES 4 TO 8

1 (15.5-ounce) can black beans, drained and rinsed

1 cup salsa or pico de gallo (heat of your choosing, though my kids prefer mild)

1 garlic clove, minced

½ teaspoon salt, plus more for seasoning

2 avocados, pitted, peeled, and cut into bite-size cubes

½ bunch fresh cilantro, chopped, plus more for garnish

1 tablespoon fresh lemon juice

4 to 8 corn tortillas (depending on how many you are serving)

4 to 8 large eggs (depending on how many you are serving)

1 tablespoon distilled white vinegar

Sour cream (optional)

1 cup shredded or crumbled queso fresco or blanco

½ teaspoon chili powder

Freshly ground black pepper

Note: Queso fresco or blanco are white cheeses found in the Spanish food section, or you can substitute with Kraft's shredded 4-cheese Mexican mix.

DURING THE WEEK, I'm usually already on my way to work early and miss out on all the "fun" getting the kids fed and out the door. But I more than make up for those mornings with weekend brunch, our favorite meal of the week, when we can all be together cooking and kicking back. Of course, Josh and Luke are always angling for sweet treats like Nutella pancakes or waffles. But as a result of our move to California, we're discovering new favorites like these delicious Huevos Rancheros. They are so good and can be eaten for breakfast, lunch, or dinner.

I usually poach the eggs, but they can be fried sunny-side up if you prefer; just don't overcook them. You want the yolk to run when you cut into the huevos. I have a four-slotted egg poacher that I use to make this dish, which saves time, and I highly recommend getting something like it. But you can poach the eggs individually as well.

1. In a saucepan, stir together the black beans, ½ cup of the salsa, the garlic, and salt. Cook over medium-high heat, stirring occasionally, until heated through, 3 to 5 minutes, then remove from the heat and set aside.

2. In a bowl, mix the avocados, cilantro, and lemon juice together like a very chunky guacamole. Season with salt.

recipe continues

3. Heat the corn tortillas on a griddle over medium heat, just long enough to warm them on each side, about 1 minute each.

4. To poach the eggs, fill a large deep skillet halfway with water and heat over medium heat just until it's lightly simmering; tiny bubbles will form. In small ramekins or separate bowls, crack each egg individually, taking care not to break the yolks. Add the vinegar to the water. Gently slide the eggs one by one into the water, leaving room between them (better not to do more than 3 at a time in a large skillet). In about 4 minutes, the whites will be cooked, and the yolk will still be soft. Use a slotted spoon to scoop up each egg and gently blot off the excess water with a paper towel.

5. To serve, place a heated tortilla on each plate. Top with 2 tablespoons of the black bean–salsa mix. Add a poached egg and top with a bit of the reserved plain salsa. Layer with a dollop of sour cream, if desired, then the avocado-cilantro mixture, and top with a healthy serving of queso fresco. Lastly, sprinkle a bit of cilantro, the chili powder and pepper over the top for an added kick and serve right away. *Buen provecho!*

SKILLET-BAKED POLENTA with Poached Egg & Tomato-Basil Salsa

GLUTEN-FREE
VEGETARIAN
SERVES 6

POLENTA

2 tablespoons unsalted butter, plus more for the skillet

Salt and freshly ground black pepper

1½ cups coarse yellow cornmeal

¼ cup heavy cream

2 tablespoons freshly grated Parmesan cheese

2 tablespoons minced fresh basil

TOMATO-BASIL SALSA

1 cup diced ripe tomatoes (plum tomatoes have the most flavor)

¼ cup chopped fresh basil

1 garlic clove, minced (optional)

1 tablespoon extra-virgin olive oil

1 teaspoon balsamic vinegar

Salt and freshly ground black pepper

1 tablespoon rice vinegar or white wine vinegar

6 large eggs (or 1 per serving)

FOR THOSE WHO EAT GLUTEN-FREE, this is a delicious and filling brunch option full of flavor and nutrients. Baked polenta is so versatile—you can top it with so many vegetables beyond what I've listed here, like sautéed mushrooms and caramelized onions, topped with Parmesan. Or sprinkle it with Italian sausage, peppers, and onions. Think of your baked polenta like a pizza crust—there are so many great combinations. So save the leftovers and enjoy for days!

1. **Make the polenta:** Preheat the oven to 350°F. Generously butter a 12-inch oven-safe or cast-iron skillet.

2. In a large saucepan, bring 4½ cups water to a boil over high heat. Season the water with salt and pepper. Reduce the heat to medium, then whisk in the cornmeal. Stirring continuously, add the cream, butter, and Parmesan. When the mixture thickens and is creamy, taste and add additional salt and pepper for flavor. Remove from the heat, then mix in the basil.

3. Pour the polenta into the skillet. Bake until firm and slightly golden, about 20 minutes. Remove from the oven and let cool slightly.

4. **Make the salsa:** In a small bowl, stir together the tomato, basil, garlic (if using), olive oil, and balsamic vinegar. Season with salt and pepper and set aside.

5. Bring a skillet of water to a boil, then reduce the heat to maintain a slow simmer and add the rice vinegar. Using a small cup,

recipe continues

one at a time, gently slide in the eggs. Cook until the whites are firm, about 4 minutes (a minute or two longer if you're cooking a large number of eggs at once), then remove with a slotted spoon and gently blot dry with a paper towel.

6. Cut the polenta into slices and top each serving with tomato salsa and a poached egg. Serve immediately.

GLUTEN-FREE OAT WAFFLES

with Mint-Berry Compote

GLUTEN-FREE
VEGETARIAN
MAKES 8 WAFFLES

MINT-BERRY COMPOTE

2 cups fresh or frozen mixed berries

3 tablespoons granulated sugar or coconut sugar

2 tablespoons chopped fresh mint

WAFFLES

2 cups oat flour

2½ teaspoons baking powder

Pinch of salt

3 large eggs, separated

1 cup milk or almond milk

6 tablespoons (¾ stick) unsalted butter, melted, or ⅓ cup coconut oil, melted

2 tablespoons pure maple syrup

1 teaspoon pure vanilla extract

Nonstick cooking spray

THERE ARE SO MANY GLUTEN-FREE FLOURS and waffle or pancake mixes out there. You can use any of those and prepare according to the box. Or you can make your own oat flour by blending gluten-free whole-grain oats (old-fashioned or quick cooking are fine) until it's a fine flour. These waffles are oh-so-good and good for you too! They are like fluffy pillows waiting to soak up the berries. You can, of course, top them with traditional maple syrup, but the berries add just the lightest touch of sweetness and pack more nutrition per bite. No guilt here, just pure deliciousness. And if you are opposed to mint, just use berries. I like to use fresh berries, but frozen work beautifully too, they just require a little more cooking time.

1. **Make the mint-berry compote:** In a medium saucepan, heat the berries and sugar over medium heat, stirring continuously. The berries will soften to a jam-like consistency and reduce to a thick syrup, 8 to 10 minutes, a few minutes more if you're using frozen. If you like it chunkier, try not to smash the berries too much; otherwise, mash the berries with a fork for a more syrupy texture.

2. Stir in the mint as the berries are almost done. Cook for 1 additional minute. Allow to cool while you make the waffles.

3. **Make the waffles:** In a large bowl, whisk together the flour, baking powder, and salt.

recipe continues

4. In another bowl, using a hand mixer, beat the egg whites until they hold soft peaks.

5. In a third bowl, mix the egg yolks, milk, melted butter, maple syrup, and vanilla.

6. Pour the wet ingredients into the dry and mix—the batter may still be lumpy—then gently fold in the egg whites. The egg whites add the fluff to the waffles.

7. Preheat the oven to 200°F. Preheat your waffle iron and spray it with nonstick spray.

8. Cook the waffles according to your waffle iron's directions, until golden brown (3 to 4 minutes on mine). Keep warm in the oven as you make the whole batch. Serve drizzled with the berry compote.

LEMON-RICOTTA PANCAKES

VEGETARIAN
MAKES ABOUT TWENTY-
FOUR 5-INCH PANCAKES

2 cups part-skim ricotta cheese

3 large eggs, separated

1½ cups all-purpose flour

¼ cup granulated sugar

2 teaspoons baking powder

¼ teaspoon baking soda

Pinch of ground nutmeg

Pinch of salt

1½ cups whole or 2% milk

1 teaspoon pure vanilla extract

1 tablespoon grated lemon zest, plus more
for garnish (from about 1 large lemon)

¼ cup fresh lemon juice

2 tablespoons unsalted butter, melted,
plus more for cooking

Fruit jam (optional)

Mint-Berry Compote
(see page 251; optional)

Pure maple syrup (optional)

THERE IS SOMETHING SO REFRESHING ABOUT THESE PANCAKES, and they are so light yet provide an excellent source of added protein with the addition of the ricotta. I top them with fresh fruit or my Mint-Berry Compote (page 251).

1. Preheat the oven to 200°F.

2. If your ricotta has too much liquid, strain it in cheesecloth over a bowl. Let it drain for about 15 minutes until it is creamier.

3. In a bowl using a hand mixer, beat the egg whites until they hold stiff peaks.

4. In a separate large bowl, whisk together the flour, granulated sugar, baking powder, baking soda, nutmeg, and salt.

5. In another large bowl, mix the ricotta, milk, egg yolks, and vanilla until well blended. Stir in the lemon zest, lemon juice, and melted butter. Mix for a minute (the batter is typically a bit lumpy, but that is fine).

6. Make a well in the dry mixture and pour the milk mixture in. Stir for another minute. Then, using a spatula, gently fold in the egg whites.

7. Heat a griddle or nonstick skillet over medium-high heat. Melt a pat of butter in the skillet and tilt the pan to spread it evenly. Ladle about ¼-cup portions of the batter into the skillet to make pancakes about 5 inches in diameter. Flip when the pancakes begin

recipe continues

to bubble on the surface and are golden and firm on the bottom, about 4 minutes, then cook on the other side for 1 to 2 minutes more. Remove the cooked pancakes and stack on a baking sheet in the oven, to keep warm until serving.

8. Serve with lemon zest, fruit jam, Mint-Berry Compote, or maple syrup, if desired.

PROTEIN-PACKED BANANA NUT BREAD

VEGETARIAN
MAKES ONE 4½ BY
8½-INCH LOAF

4 tablespoons (½ stick) unsalted butter, at room temperature, 1 tablespoon melted butter, plus more for the pan

¾ cup all-purpose flour, plus more for dusting

¾ cup sugar

2 large eggs

1 teaspoon pure vanilla extract

2 large ripe bananas

¾ cup whole wheat flour

¼ cup flax meal (optional)

1 teaspoon baking powder

½ teaspoon baking soda

1 teaspoon ground cinnamon

½ teaspoon ground nutmeg

½ teaspoon salt

½ cup chopped walnuts

¼ cup plain 2% Greek yogurt

1 tablespoon oats

THIS IS A GREAT WAY to use up those overly ripe bananas that no one ever wants. My kids love waking up to the smell of my banana bread on the weekends, and it makes for a great snack all week long (if it even lasts past the first day). It's even more delicious reheated in the microwave and topped with a light smear of butter.

Yogurt adds extra creaminess and protein, and the flax adds health benefits and some crunch, but is optional.

1. Preheat the oven to 350°F. Grease a bread pan with butter, then add a layer of parchment paper just on the bottom. Butter the parchment, then lightly flour the bottom and sides of the pan, shaking out any excess.

2. In a large bowl using a hand mixer, cream the butter, sugar, eggs, and vanilla. Add the bananas, mashing them up and mixing until fully blended.

3. In a separate large bowl, whisk together the flours, flax meal (if using), baking powder, baking soda, cinnamon, nutmeg, and salt. Stir in the nuts.

4. Add the egg-banana mixture to the dry ingredients and mix until all is evenly blended. Add the yogurt and stir until just blended.

5. Pour the batter into the prepared pan and sprinkle the top evenly with the oats.

6. Bake for about 40 minutes, checking it at 35 minutes. When it is golden brown, the top splits like a bread loaf, and a toothpick inserted into the center comes out clean, it is done.

7. Brush the top lightly with the melted butter and enjoy!

STRAWBERRY YOGURT CRÈME with Vanilla Biscuits & Granola

VEGETARIAN
MAKES ABOUT 16

BISCUITS

½ cup (1 stick) unsalted butter, frozen, plus 2 tablespoons unsalted butter, melted

2½ cups white self-rising flour (White Lily or King Arthur are preferred, as they're the lightest), plus more for dusting

1 tablespoon sugar

½ teaspoon pure vanilla extract

1¼ cups very cold buttermilk

STRAWBERRY YOGURT CRÈME

½ cup heavy cream

2 tablespoons sugar

½ teaspoon pure vanilla extract

1 cup plain 2% Greek yogurt

1 cup minced fresh strawberries

Granola, store-bought or homemade (page 38), for garnish

I BELIEVE THIS RECIPE WILL BE A WEEKEND BRUNCH FAVORITE in your home as much as it is in mine. The key is the flaky and truly delicious biscuit. Start by learning how to make the biscuits, then you can add all the extras. While my kids love the biscuit plain, I add strawberry crème yogurt and granola to give them a more protein-packed and filling brunch meal. If you want to save some time, you can make the biscuits ahead and just freeze once they have baked. Wrap the biscuits in parchment paper and reheat in the oven when you want to serve them again.

1. **Make the biscuits:** Preheat the oven to 450°F. Line a baking sheet with parchment paper.

2. Cut the frozen butter into ¼-inch cubes or use the large holes of a box grater to grate the butter over a piece of parchment paper.

3. Put the flour in a large bowl and incorporate the butter, mixing gently with your hands. Add the sugar and vanilla, mixing just briefly with your hands. Cover and refrigerate the dough for about 10 minutes to keep the butter extra cold (this makes the biscuits flaky).

4. Make a well in the center and pour in the buttermilk. Using a wooden spoon, stir until the buttermilk is incorporated into the dry ingredients.

recipe continues

5. On a lightly floured surface, use a floured rolling pin to roll the dough out into a rectangle. Sprinkle the top of the dough and the pin with additional flour if it's a bit sticky. Fold the dough in half and roll again. Do this four or five times, until all the ingredients are mixed in.

6. Roll the dough out to ½ inch thick. Dip the cutting edge of a biscuit cutter or a glass cup around 3½ inches in diameter into flour, then press into the dough to form the biscuits (do not twist, as this will affect how much the biscuit rises). Repeat this process for all the biscuits. Re-form and roll any dough scraps to make a couple more.

7. Arrange the biscuits on the lined baking sheet, setting them next to one another so they touch. Bake until golden on top, about 12 minutes. Brush the top of each biscuit with the melted butter, then transfer to a wire rack to cool a little bit while you make the strawberry yogurt crème.

8. Make the strawberry yogurt crème: In a glass bowl using a hand mixer, whip the cream, sugar, and vanilla until it holds stiff peaks. Add the yogurt and strawberries and whisk until incorporated.

9. Split open the biscuits and fill with generous spoonfuls of the strawberry yogurt crème. Garnish with a sprinkle of granola and serve.

The Sweet Stuff

Honestly, I admit I'm not a big dessert baker or maker; but I do love a sweet treat after dinner. I try to avoid making the really decadent stuff too often, because I have a tremendous sweet tooth and I'm the one who ends up eating it. My kids, shockingly, don't have a big sweet tooth (where did these kids come from?). That said, I do think it's a good idea to have a battery of good signature dessert recipes that you can rely on. Again, a lot of my inspiration comes from my youth or travels, from desserts I've savored around the world, or that have a healthful twist (sorry!). Yes, even the delicious can sometimes be good for you!

ALL THINGS FLAN

THERE IS NOTHING MY MOM MAKES BETTER, IN MY OPINION, THAN HER FLAN. This is one of those recipes that has been passed down and is almost a family heirloom. (Here's where the osmosis comes in.) It's amazing how one dessert can mean so much and bring forth so many memories. That's what I love about certain foods: they take you on a journey to a place and time, or even just allow you to feel the comforts of home.

Back to the flan: This is truly one of the easiest desserts I make, but the trick is caramelizing the sugar just right. Don't be intimidated by using a double boiler or baking using a water bath; it's beyond simple once you've tried it. I've "skinnied" this recipe up a bit, using low-fat sweetened condensed milk or low-fat evaporated milk—and I honestly can't tell the difference. Once you've mastered the original, you'll find it's a forgiving recipe. But the recipe will work using the full-fat versions, if you prefer. Try the coconut variation, or for the holidays, try my pumpkin version—or experiment by adding mango puree for a tropical flan, or chocolate for a winter flan. You can't go wrong.

BASIC FLAN

SERVES 8

6 large eggs

1 (12-ounce) can low-fat evaporated milk

1 (14-ounce) can low-fat or fat-free sweetened condensed milk

1 teaspoon pure vanilla extract

¾ cup sugar

1. Preheat the oven to 350°F. Fill a roasting pan one-quarter of the way with water and set it in the oven.

2. In a blender, combine the eggs, evaporated and condensed milks, and vanilla. Blend until smooth and set aside.

3. Scoop the sugar into a small saucepan. Over very low heat, slowly caramelize the sugar. This is the hardest part of the recipe because the key is not to let the sugar burn or get too dark. The pan can be directly over the heat, but it gets very, very hot, so use a potholder. Using a wooden spoon, work the sugar around the pan until it starts to liquefy. Remove from the heat as soon as the sugar starts to turns a light caramel color.

4. Immediately pour the caramelized sugar into a round glass baking dish, such as a 9-inch Pyrex pie dish. Tilt the dish to coat the bottom and sides with the caramel.

5. Pour the custard mixture into the caramel-coated dish. Place it in the water-filled roasting pan in the oven.

6. Bake for about 45 minutes, but as ovens can vary, start checking for doneness after 30 minutes. The flan is cooked through when the top pulls from the sides of the baking dish a bit or when the top is firm and a toothpick inserted into the center comes out clean.

7. Remove from the oven and set aside to cool to room temperature, then refrigerate for at least 4 hours.

8. To serve, take a large dessert platter and place it over the baking dish as if it were a lid. Do this over the sink to ensure no spillage. Quickly flip the pan and the platter together. The flan should come out of the baking dish perfectly, topped with a beautiful caramel glaze. Enjoy!

Double Boiler Method

1. In a blender, combine the eggs, evaporated and condensed milks, and vanilla. Blend until smooth and set aside.

2. Fill the bottom of a double boiler about a quarter of the way full with water and set over medium heat.

3. Scoop the sugar into the top of the double boiler. Over a very low flame or low heat, slowly caramelize the sugar as directed in Step 3.

4. Coat all sides of the double boiler top with the caramel by rotating the pan in a circular motion.

5. Pour the custard mixture into the caramel-coated pan. Set it over the bottom of the double boiler.

6. Cook for about 45 minutes, but check the water level in the base every 15 minutes or so to ensure it's always about one-quarter full. The flan is cooked through when the top pulls from the sides of the pan a bit or when the top is firm and a toothpick inserted into the center comes out clean.

7. Set aside to cool to room temperature, then refrigerate for at least 4 hours.

8. To serve, take a large dessert platter and place it over the top of the double-boiler top as if it were a lid. Do this over the sink to ensure no spillage. Quickly flip the pan and the platter together. The flan should come out of the mold perfectly topped with a beautiful caramel glaze.

COCONUT FLAN

SERVES 8

6 large eggs

1 (14-ounce) can low-fat or fat-free sweetened condensed milk

1 cup low-fat evaporated milk

½ cup light coconut milk

½ cup unsweetened coconut flakes

1 teaspoon pure vanilla extract

¾ cup sugar

Follow the same method as for the basic flan, adding the coconut milk and coconut flakes with the eggs, milk, and vanilla.

PUMPKIN FLAN

SERVES 8

4 large eggs

1 (12-ounce) can low-fat evaporated milk

1 (14-ounce) can low-fat or fat-free sweetened condensed milk

1 cup canned pure pumpkin puree (such as Libby's)

1 teaspoon pure vanilla extract

1 teaspoon ground cinnamon

½ teaspoon ground nutmeg

¾ cup sugar

Follow the same method as for the basic flan, just using fewer eggs and adding the pumpkin puree, cinnamon, and nutmeg with the eggs, milk, and vanilla.

[COCONUT FLAN]

[PUMPKIN FLAN]

ROMEO & JULIET (Goiabada with Cheese)

VEGETARIAN

MAKES 15

Store-bought frozen puff pastry sheets, or 1 package prepared mini puff pastry shells

All-purpose flour, for dusting (optional)

5 ounces guava paste

5 ounces queso fresco

IN BRAZIL THIS PERFECT PAIRING is known as *Romeu e Julieta*—a fresh, white farmers' cheese (typically *queijo mineiro*—it's like a firm cottage cheese) served thinly sliced and topped with a slice of guava paste. Often it is served at breakfast with a side of toast or bread, or for dessert. Here, I nest them in puff pastry.

1. Thaw the frozen puff pastry by placing it in the refrigerator for 4 to 6 hours.

2. Preheat the oven to 400°F.

3. If you are using a puff pastry sheet, unfold it on a lightly floured surface. Lightly grease a mini-muffin tin.

4. Using a 2-inch round or square pastry cutter or a sharp knife, cut the dough into fifteen 2-inch rounds or squares (this will use almost half a sheet). Shape them in the mini muffin tins. If square, point the corners up. Poke a few holes in the bottom of each cup with a fork. If your pastry shells are pre-formed and not already baked, separate them and arrange them on an ungreased baking sheet.

5. Bake the shells for about 10 minutes.

6. Slice the guava paste into fifteen ¾ by ¾ by ½-inch squares and the cheese into fifteen 1 by 1 by ½-inch cubes.

7. Using a small spoon, press each shell down in the center to create a well. In each shell, put a cheese cube on the bottom and then a guava paste square on top. Return them to the oven and bake, checking frequently, until the pastry turns a golden brown, 8 to 10 minutes more.

8. Gently remove each pastry from the pan with a utensil so they do not break and let cool to room temperature before serving.

GREEK YOGURT with Pistachio, Honey & Shredded Wheat

VEGETARIAN
SERVES 4

2 cups full-fat or 2% plain Greek yogurt

¼ cup honey

½ cup crumbled plain Shredded Wheat

¼ cup chopped pistachios

Note: Start to finish, this dessert should take less than 5 minutes. Oh, and it's not just dessert! It also makes for a healthy breakfast, packing in all the right nutrition to get you started on your day.

THIS IS ONE OF MY ALL-TIME FAVORITE healthy, sweet treats. I would rather have this Greek yogurt dessert than a piece of cake, honestly, and you don't have to feel guilty, as it's packed with protein, probiotics, and good-for-you Shredded Wheat. Now, if you want a little indulgence, go for creamy full-fat Greek yogurt, but I also think the 2-percent fat yogurt tastes just as good; it is just a tiny bit tangier. Once you add the honey, you won't be able to tell the difference, and it's still perfection.

1. Dole out ½ cup of yogurt into each of four dessert or ice cream bowls. Drizzle 1 tablespoon of the honey over each serving.

2. Sprinkle 1 to 2 tablespoons of the Shredded Wheat over the honey. Add up to 1 tablespoon of the finely chopped pistachios (depending how nutty you like it).

3. Serve right away, and swirl all the ingredients together for the best bites!

BERRY PARFAIT with Coconut Granola Crumble

VEGETARIAN
MAKES 2 PARFAITS

2 cups frozen or fresh mixed berries

2 tablespoons sugar

½ teaspoon grated lemon zest

2 tablespoons fresh lemon juice

2 cups full-fat or 2% plain Greek yogurt

Coconut Granola (page 38)

2 teaspoons unsweetened shredded coconut, for garnish (optional)

ONCE AGAIN, THE STAR OF THIS DESSERT is the Greek yogurt, but with a berry compote and the granola crumble, it almost tastes like a heavenly slice of cheesecake with a berry topping. I like to make this in a sundae cup with all the layers, which helps make it feel like a decadent dessert. Perception is everything, after all.

1. In a saucepan, combine the berries, sugar, lemon zest, and lemon juice. Bring the mixture to a simmer over medium heat and cook until the berries release their juices, 5 to 7 minutes for frozen berries, about 3 minutes for fresh. Allow the berries to gently boil, then reduce the heat to a low simmer and cook until the sauce thickens into a syrup, 2 to 3 minutes more.

2. Remove the compote from the heat and set it aside to cool to room temperature.

3. In a cup or sundae bowl, put a tablespoon or two of the berry compote. Next add a layer of the yogurt, and then a layer of the granola. Repeat the layers, adding more compote, yogurt, and granola. Repeat to make a second parfait.

4. Top with a drizzle of compote and a sprinkle of the shredded coconut, if you are a coconut fan like me. Cover with plastic wrap and refrigerate until you are ready for this wholesome goodness, or enjoy right away.

GINGER-PEACH SORBET

GLUTEN-FREE
VEGETARIAN
SERVES 8 TO 10

¾ cup honey (or ⅔ cup sugar, if vegan)

2 pounds frozen or 6 or 7 peeled
and pitted fresh peaches

½ cup full-fat coconut milk

2 tablespoons chopped fresh ginger

Grated zest of 1 lime

1 tablespoon fresh lime juice

1 teaspoon pure vanilla extract

Fresh mint, for garnish

THIS IS ONE OF THE FRESHEST and lightest desserts or summertime snacks. The combination of peaches and ginger is a pairing that gives you just the right amount of sweetness and zest to cleanse your palate. You can make this all year long, using frozen peaches when you don't have fresh. Also, this is a great base recipe to use when experimenting with other fruit sorbets . . . instead of peaches, try using frozen mangoes or strawberries and bananas, or a combination of fruits to your liking.

1. In a small saucepan, combine 1 cup water and the honey over medium heat and stir until the honey dissolves.

2. In a blender or food processor, combine the peaches, coconut milk, ginger, lime zest, lime juice, vanilla, and honey syrup and blend until smooth.

3. Portion out into individual serving dishes, then freeze for 4 to 6 hours (or pour into a larger container and freeze).

4. When fully frozen, garnish with a fresh sprig of mint and serve.

SUMMER BERRY TARTE TATIN

VEGETARIAN
SERVES 6 TO 8

DOUGH

5 tablespoons unsalted butter, cut into small cubes and chilled

¾ cup all-purpose flour, plus more for dusting

¼ cup whole wheat flour

1 tablespoon sugar

Pinch of salt

1 large egg yolk

2 tablespoons ice water

1 teaspoon apple cider vinegar (this makes the crust flakier)

FILLING

¼ cup sugar

1 tablespoon fresh lemon juice

1 teaspoon pure vanilla extract

3 tablespoons unsalted butter

8 ounces fresh strawberries, halved

8 ounces fresh raspberries, half chopped and half left whole

4 ounces fresh blackberries

I JUST LOVE PIE, especially in the summer, using the most seasonal fruits Mother Nature has to offer. This berry tarte tatin is lightened up a bit, as I don't use a lot of sweetener; the berries are plenty sweet. I also make a blended whole wheat crust, which I love, but if you prefer traditional, use only white flour instead of the whole wheat. (You may use store-bought pie dough as well if you want to save some time.)

Typically a tarte tatin is an upside-down pie, which you flip when ready to serve. This keeps the crust really golden and flaky. What I like about this recipe is that it is very rustic, and that's the appeal: no need for perfection.

Serve with a dollop of crème fraîche, light whipped cream, or frozen yogurt.

---

1. **Make the dough:** In a large bowl (or in a food processor, but it's quick and I think a bit better by hand), combine the butter, flours, sugar, and salt, using your fingers, until the butter is distributed throughout, smaller than pea size. Add the egg yolk, ice water, and vinegar and stir using a spatula or wooden spoon, until the dough has just come together—do not overwork it. (It's similar to a shortbread dough.)

2. Dump the dough onto a floured surface and form it into a disc; add more flour or water, if the dough seems too sticky or too dry. Wrap it in plastic wrap and refrigerate for at least 2 hours or up to 2 days.

3. Preheat the oven to 400°F.

recipe continues

4. Make the filling: In a small saucepan, stir together the sugar, 1 tablespoon water, the lemon juice, and vanilla over medium heat. Stir gently until the mixture simmers and cook until it is the color of a light caramel, being careful not to let the syrup get too dark, about 5 minutes. Carefully stir in the butter (watch out, as it may spatter), and continue stirring until the sauce is smooth. Pour the caramel syrup into an 8- to 10-inch oven-safe skillet, pie dish, or cake form, tilting it to coat the bottom.

5. Arrange the strawberries, whole raspberries, and blackberries in a concentric pattern over the bottom of the dish. Fill in the gaps with the chopped raspberries.

6. When the dough is sufficiently chilled, roll it out into a circle that is about 1 inch larger in diameter than the skillet or dish.

7. Lay the dough on top of the fruit filling, then tuck the sides inside the pan or baking dish. Using a paring knife, cut four 1-inch slits across the top to release steam as it bakes.

8. Bake the tarte until it is lightly browned and the berries are bubbling, 25 to 30 minutes.

9. Remove the tarte from the oven and let cool for 15 to 20 minutes.

10. Take a large round plate and place it on top of the tarte tatin. Over the sink, hold the plate and tarte dish or pan together tightly and flip them over quickly. The idea is to keep the juices as much on the plate as possible and the berries in place, but don't stress too much—this is meant to be rustic! Serve right away.

Notes: If you are making your own crust, keep the ingredients well chilled. Also, try to serve the tarte soon after flipping it, as the juices will be flowing and will make the otherwise crispy crust soggy. • You can make the dough up to 2 days in advance. If more time is needed, it also freezes well; just allow enough time for thawing it fully before rolling and baking.

LIGHTENED-UP COCONUT CREAM PIE

VEGETARIAN
SERVES 8 TO 10

CRUST

1 cup raw almonds

1 cup old-fashioned oats

5 tablespoons coconut oil, melted, plus more if needed

3 tablespoons honey

1 teaspoon pure vanilla extract

½ teaspoon ground cinnamon

Pinch of salt

FILLING AND TOPPING

3 tablespoons honey

1 large egg

1 egg yolk

1 teaspoon pure vanilla extract

Pinch of salt

3 tablespoons cornstarch

1½ cups light coconut milk

½ cup shredded unsweetened coconut (or sweetened, if you prefer), plus 3 tablespoons for topping

1 cup whipped topping (such as light Cool Whip or Truwhip)

IF YOU LOVE COCONUT AS MUCH AS I DO, this dessert is just heaven. It's very hard to lighten up this classic without sacrificing too much of its creamy texture and flavor. This recipe is a slightly better-for-you version, with a nutty crust and some lighter substitutions. However, let's be real: a little coconut cream pie goes a long way, so just lighten up your portions and enjoy! (Though my husband can and has eaten a whole pie practically by himself.)

1. **Make the crust:** Preheat the oven to 350°F.

2. In a food processor, combine the almonds and oats and process well into a flour.

3. Add the coconut oil, honey, vanilla, cinnamon, and salt. Pulse until it forms a dough. Scrape down the sides and add more coconut oil if it is too dry.

4. Press the dough into a pie dish, forming it like a graham cracker crust, until the bottom and sides are evenly covered.

5. Bake the crust for 12 to 15 minutes, until golden. Remove and let cool.

6. **Make the filling and topping:** In a bowl, whisk the honey, egg, egg yolk, vanilla, and salt. Whisk in the cornstarch.

recipe continues

7. In a saucepan, gently heat the coconut milk and ½ cup of the shredded coconut over medium-low heat until the milk is hot but not boiling. Add the egg mixture and cook, stirring continuously, until it has thickened to a custard consistency, about 4 minutes. Remove from the heat and let cool for about 30 minutes, stirring once or twice.

8. Pour the custard into the prepared piecrust and refrigerate until it is somewhat firm, like a pudding.

9. Preheat the oven to 350°F. Line a baking sheet with parchment paper.

10. Spread the remaining 3 tablespoons shredded coconut over the lined baking sheet and toast them in the oven. Check periodically and stir frequently to toast the coconut evenly, until golden, about 8 minutes.

11. When you are ready to serve, top the custard with the whipped topping and sprinkle with the toasted coconut.

TRES LECHES CUPCAKES

CAKE
Vegetable oil, for the cupcake pan(s)

5 large eggs, separated

1 cup granulated sugar

½ cup (1 stick) unsalted butter, cut into pieces

1½ cups all-purpose flour

1 teaspoon baking powder

½ teaspoon salt

½ teaspoon pure vanilla extract

2 cups whole milk

1 (14-ounce) can full-fat sweetened condensed milk

1 (12-ounce) can 2% evaporated milk

WHIPPED TOPPING
1 cup heavy cream

¼ cup powdered sugar

½ teaspoon pure vanilla extract

Ground cinnamon or shaved chocolate, for garnish

Thinly sliced strawberries, for garnish (optional)

THIS RECIPE IS INSPIRED by the classic Latin cake, which is one of my favorites. *Tres leches*, or "three milks," is literally that: sweetened condensed milk, evaporated milk, and regular milk, making for a very moist and delicious cake. This can be made as a large cake, but making cupcakes means better portion control!

1. Preheat the oven to 350°F. Grease two 6-cup cupcake pans or one 12-cup pan with vegetable oil.

2. In a large bowl using a hand mixer, cream the egg yolks with ½ cup of the granulated sugar. Add the butter pieces and beat until evenly incorporated into the yolk mixture.

3. Gradually beat in the flour, then the baking powder, salt, and vanilla, mixing until a smooth batter forms.

4. In a separate bowl using a hand mixer with clean beaters, beat the egg whites with the remaining ½ cup granulated sugar until light and fluffy.

5. Gently fold the egg whites into the batter, a little a time. This allows the cake to remain spongy and fluffy.

6. Pour the batter into the prepared cupcake pans and bake until the tops are golden and a toothpick inserted into the center of a cupcake comes out clean, about 25 minutes. Let cool in the pans on a wire rack for 5 minutes.

recipe continues

Note: If you have extra sweet milk mixture, freeze it in ice cube trays and serve them to the kids in glasses of milk for a sweet iced treat.

7. While the cupcakes are baking, mix the whole milk, condensed milk, and evaporated milk in a blender, then chill the mixture in the refrigerator for at least 1 hour.

8. When the milks are very cold and the cupcakes have cooled but are still warm, gently remove them from the cupcake pans and arrange them on a small rimmed baking sheet. Poke the top of each cupcake with a fork several times, then pour a table-spoon of the milk mixture on top of each cupcake. Repeat with 2 tablespoons more per cupcake. Let the cupcakes rest for a few minutes in the milk that has run off onto the pan until it has been absorbed and moistened the cake. Even better, dip the bottoms of each cupcake in the milk mixture, as you really want to drench the cakes in it to make them super moist (the cake is on the dry side for this purpose). Place them back in the cupcake pans and refrigerate until you are ready to serve. Reserve and refrigerate any extra milk mixture for serving.

9. **Make the whipped topping:** Just before serving, in a large bowl, whip the heavy cream until it starts to thicken, then add the powdered sugar and vanilla until the cream holds soft peaks (don't overwhip, as it will become too creamy).

10. When ready to serve, remove the cupcakes from the pans. Spoon the whipped cream on top of the cupcakes and spread to frost, then add a sprinkle of cinnamon on top. Top each with a slice of strawberry, if desired. Plate them individually on small plates or in small bowls, and spoon a little more of the milk mix-ture on the plate or in the bowl as a sweet sauce.

VANILLA MILK ICE POPS

GLUTEN-FREE
VEGETARIAN
SERVES 6

1 (14-ounce) can 2% evaporated milk

½ (12-ounce) can full-fat sweetened condensed milk

1 teaspoon pure vanilla extract

MY MOM WOULD MAKE THESE INCREDIBLE ICE POPS for us all the time when we were kids. They are so delicious and easy to make, with just three ingredients. I have so many childhood memories eating these vanilla ice pops. My older sister and I would sit outside licking away, and I'd always try to make mine last a little longer than hers so I could still have a bit left when her pop was gone. This is one childhood recipe I continue to make for my boys, who think these ice pops are better than ice cream (and I know they are lighter and a bit healthier than ice cream, so it's a win-win).

1. In a medium bowl, stir together all the ingredients.

2. Pour the mixture into 6 ice pop forms and freeze until solid.

3. To remove from the forms, run the sides of the forms under warm water, then gently pull out the ice pops. Enjoy!

ACKNOWLEDGMENTS

This book was lovingly conceived and created with my family's support. To Joe, thanks for always being willing to taste test and for being the most positive person I know. To my beautiful boys, Josh and Luke, you are my pride and joy, and I love every adventure life brings us because it makes us stronger. I would not have been able to put all this together were it not for my muse, my mom, who always inspires me in the kitchen and in life. Thanks for showing me the way, Mom! To my dad and sisters who also have taught me always to try new things and never be afraid of a good challenge. To Patty, thanks for always being our family's backbone! I wouldn't be able to do any of this without all your help.

To my TV families at the *TODAY* show and *Access Hollywood*, thank you for an incredible journey and for helping me realize my dreams.

Finally to an incredible team, who helped taste test, design, and collaborate in all things having to do with *At Home with Natalie*. To Ann, thank you for the many revisions and for your sharp eye and taste buds (and thanks to your family for enduring the "testing"). Justin, thanks for giving me this incredible opportunity to bring these wonderful memories to life. To my agents, Jon and Andy, thanks for getting me out of my comfort zone and for working so hard for me. And to our design team, Alanna, Carrie, and Ethel, I am in awe of all of you! What a fun week we had at my house cooking, chatting, and creating this beautiful book that my family will always treasure.

INDEX